e.explore

Space Travel

LONDON, NEW YORK, MELBOURNE,
MUNICH and DELHI

Author Ian Graham

Senior Editor Jayne Miller
Project Editor Robert Dinwiddie
Weblink Editors Clare Lister, Mariza O' Keeffe,
Roger Brownlie, John Bennett

Managing Editor Camilla Hallinan

Digital Development Manager Fergus Day
DTP Technical Adviser Toby Beedell
DTP Co-ordinator Sarah Pfitzner
Production Erica Rosen

Category Publisher Sue Grabham

Consultant Peter Bond

Senior Designers Owen Peyton Jones, Smiljka Surla, Yumiko Tahata
Illustrators Mark Longworth, Darren Poore
Cartography Simon Mumford

Managing Art Editor Sophia M Tampakopoulos Turner

Picture Researcher Fran Vargo
Picture Librarians Sarah Mills, Karl Strange, Kate Ledwith
Jacket Neal Cobourne

Art Director Simon Webb

First published in Great Britain in 2004
by Dorling Kindersley Limited, 80 Strand, London WC2R 0RL

Penguin Group

Copyright © 2004 Dorling Kindersley Limited

Google™ is a trademark of Google Technology Inc.

2 4 6 8 10 9 7 5 3 1

A CIP catalogue for this book is available from the British Library.

ISBN 1 4053 0361 1

Colour reproduction by Colourscan, Singapore
Printed in China by Toppan Printing Co. (Shenzen) Ltd.

Discover more at
www.dk.com

e.explore

Space Travel

Written by **Ian Graham**

How to use the e.explore website

e.explore Space Travel has its own website, created by DK and Google™. When you look up a subject in the book, the article gives you key facts and displays a keyword that links you to extra information online. Just follow these easy steps.

http://www.spacetravel.dke-explore.com

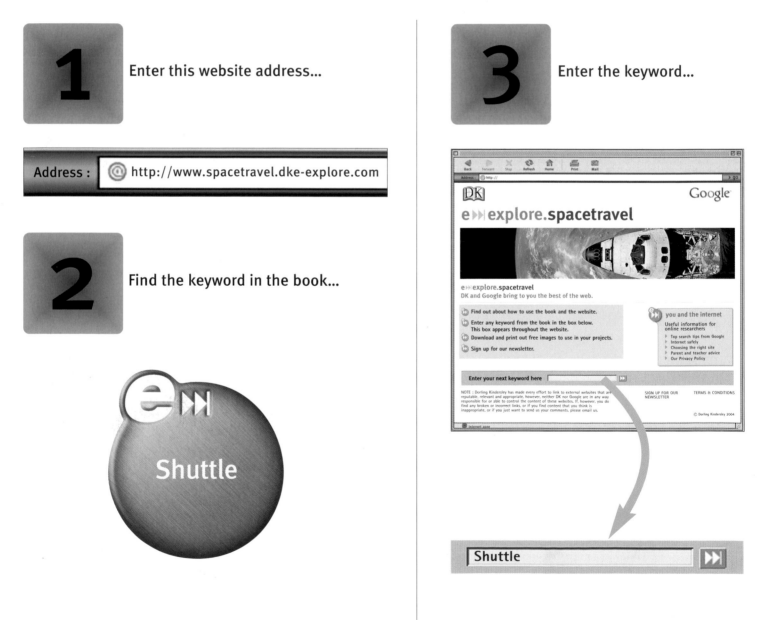

1 Enter this website address...

Address : @ http://www.spacetravel.dke-explore.com

2 Find the keyword in the book...

Shuttle

3 Enter the keyword...

Shuttle

You can only use the keywords from the book to search on our website for the specially selected DK/Google links.

Be safe while you are online:

- Always get permission from an adult before connecting to the internet.

- Never give out personal information about yourself.

- Never arrange to meet someone you have talked to online.

- If a site asks you to log in with your name or email address, ask permission from an adult first.

- Do not reply to emails from strangers – tell an adult.

Parents: Dorling Kindersley actively and regularly reviews and updates the links. However, content may change. Dorling Kindersley is not responsible for any site but its own. We recommend that children are supervised while online, that they do not use Chat Rooms, and that filtering software is used to block unsuitable material.

---

4 Click on your chosen link...

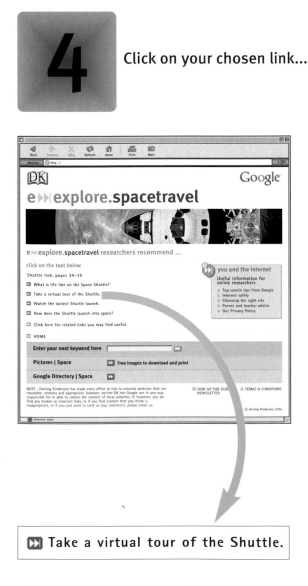

▶▶ Take a virtual tour of the Shuttle.

Links include animations, videos, sound buttons, virtual tours, interactive quizzes, databases, timelines, and realtime reports.

5 Download fantastic pictures...

Pictures | Space ▶▶

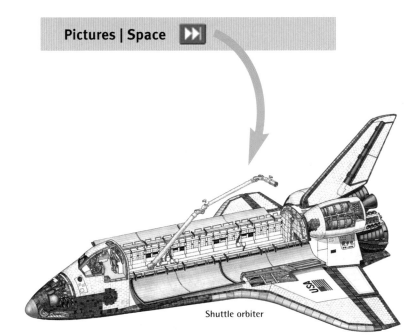

Shuttle orbiter

The pictures are free of charge, but can be used for personal non-commercial use only.

Go back to the book for your next subject...

WHY EXPLORE SPACE?

People have gazed up at the night sky for thousands of years and wondered what the countless wandering points of light were. Improved technology means we can observe and explore further into the Universe. Just as ancient explorers travelled across uncharted lands and oceans to see what was there, modern explorers venture into space. By studying space, scientists can discover what is out there, find out how the Universe began, and learn more about Earth.

SATURN AS SEEN THROUGH A TELESCOPE

Eyepiece - observer looks through the eyepiece lens, which magnifies the image

Telescope tube moves in and out to bring the image into sharp focus

Main mirror captures light from objects and reflects it onto the side of the tube

astronomy

◄ NEWTON'S REFLECTOR TELESCOPE
English scientist Sir Isaac Newton invented a new type of telescope in 1668. Telescopes had been used to see further into the Universe since Italian astronomer Galileo turned one to the sky in 1609. The first telescopes used glass lenses to gather light from the sky and bend it to a focus. They bent different colours of light unequally, so the image was distorted. Newton's telescope used mirrors to capture the light and reflect it, without bending it. This produced clearer images. The giant telescopes used today can trace their ancestry back to Newton's reflector.

THE MILKY WAY ►
Our Sun is just one of more than 100 billion stars that travel through space together in a swirling flattened spiral called the Milky Way galaxy. If the sky is clear and dark enough, you might be able to see a bright band stretching across it. You are looking edgewise through the galaxy. The Milky Way is so big that if you could travel at the speed of light, 300,000 km per second (186,411 miles per second), it would take 100,000 years to cross it.

▲ LOOKING DEEPER INTO SPACE
When astronomers look into space with powerful modern telescopes, they see fuzzy regions called nebulae. Many are vast clouds of gas and dust where new stars form. The Eskimo Nebula is made from gas thrown out into space by a dying star. It is about 2,930 light years from Earth. One light year is about 9.5 million million km (5.9 million million miles).

◄ GIANT TELESCOPES
Observatories, such as the Keck Observatory in Hawaii, help astronomers to explore beyond the atmosphere and into space. Each of the twin Keck telescopes uses a mirror 10 m (30 ft) across to collect starlight. Earth's atmosphere distorts the light from stars, so most telescopes are built on mountains above the thickest part of the atmosphere. Keck is 4,205 m (14,700 ft) above sea level on top of Mauna Kea.

▲ EYES IN SPACE

Some objects in the Universe give off X-rays. These are invisible beams of radiation from areas far hotter than the Sun, such as clusters of galaxies or the remains of stars that have exploded. Telescopes designed to receive X-rays have to be sent into space to work, as X-rays from space do not reach Earth. The Chandra X-ray telescope (above) is a space telescope. Chandra is powerful enough to see something as small as a full-stop at a distance of nearly 20 km (12 miles).

◄ PICTURING X-RAYS

When the Chandra X-ray telescope observed a distant galaxy called NGC 4631, its images showed a cloud of hot gas all around it. The galaxy is about 25 light years away, but it is similar to our own Milky Way. Scientists have wondered for nearly 50 years whether the Milky Way was surrounded by a cloud of hot gas. Chandra's observations may help scientists to find out.

CAMERAS IN SPACE ►

Space probes sent out from Earth to explore the planets and their moons carry cameras to take close-up pictures. Compare this image of the ringed planet Saturn, to the view seen through an ordinary telescope at the top of page 8. Probes have shown us craters on Mercury, the poisonous atmosphere around Venus, huge canyons on Mars, and volcanoes erupting on one of Jupiter's moons. Each photograph contains valuable information for scientists to study.

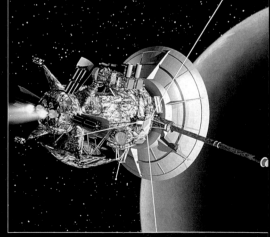

ROBOTIC SPACE EXPLORERS ▲

We cannot yet travel to all of the planets that circle the Sun in our Solar System. Instead, we send spacecraft to do it for us. Space probes spend years crossing oceans of space to distant worlds. The Cassini spacecraft took seven years to reach Saturn. Nearly everything we know about the planets and their moons has been discovered by unmanned space probes. These robots are the explorers of the 21st century.

VENUS   MARS
MERCURY   EARTH
SUN   JUPITER   SATURN
URANUS   NEPTUNE   PLUTO

◄ PLANETARY FORCES
All the planets and their moons exert a gravitational pull on spacecraft, although this pull is quite weak until a craft gets fairly close to the planet. For craft flying through the outer Solar System, the gravity of the largest planet, Jupiter, has the biggest effect. Gravity can help an interplanetary spacecraft to reach its destination. Some probes save fuel by using one planet's gravity to accelerate them towards the next planet.

◄ SUN'S EFFECTS
The Sun affects spacecraft in many ways. First, its enormous gravity pulls them towards it. Second, it heats a spacecraft and bathes it in potentially harmful radiation. Third, sunlight striking a spacecraft exerts a tiny push on the craft. Big spacecraft are affected the most, because the sunlight acts over a larger area. The effect tends to make a spacecraft drift off-course. From time to time, its engines may have to be fired to bring it back onto the correct flight-path.

FLYING IN SPACE

The laws of nature that govern spaceflight were written down by the scientist Sir Isaac Newton (1642-1727) 300 years ago. Scientists who plan spaceflights today use his law of gravitation and his laws of motion to plot a spacecraft's course through space. These laws are simple, but calculating a spacecraft's flight-path is difficult. The planets and spacecraft are all moving in different directions at different speeds, so the sizes and directions of the many forces acting on a spacecraft are constantly changing.

⑤ *Exosphere is a region that extends beyond a height of 500 km (310 miles) above Earth's surface.*

④ *Thermosphere extends to a height of about 500 km (310 miles) above Earth's surface.*

③ *Mesosphere is 50-85 km (30-55 miles) above Earth's surface.*

② *Stratosphere is a calm layer stretching to about 50 km (30 miles) above the ground.*

① *Troposphere extends to 6 km (4 miles) above the poles and 11 km (8 miles) above the equator.*

LEAVING THE ATMOSPHERE ►
An Ariane rocket powers its way up through the atmosphere. Boosters give the maximum power necessary to lift the rocket off the ground. The vehicle accelerates slowly at the beginning of its flight, when it is at its heaviest. As the rocket rapidly burns fuel, it becomes lighter. The lighter it is, the faster it accelerates. It climbs vertically at first and then tilts over further and further until it is flying horizontally as it reaches its orbital height.

▲ LAYERS OF THE ATMOSPHERE
Earth's atmosphere is about 500 km (310 miles) deep, but has no sharp boundary, fading into space as it gets thinner in the layer called the exosphere. Spacecraft have to pass through the atmosphere to get to space. While satellites and space probes are boosted through the lowest part of the atmosphere, where the air is densest, they are enclosed in a protective aerodynamic casing, called a fairing. The fairing protects the spacecraft from the air and weather outside. It also gives them a smooth, streamlined shape that allows them to slip easily through the air.

GOING INTO ORBIT

When a rocket is used to blast an object into space, the result depends on how much horizontal speed the object is given. If the speed is relatively small (for example 8,000 kph or 5,000 mph), Earth's gravity will soon pull the object back to the ground. Such a flight is called suborbital. The greater the speed the object is given, the further it will go before it reaches the ground. If it is given a speed of about 28,000 kph (17,400 mph), the object never reaches the ground but goes right round Earth – in other words, into orbit.

Rocket

Suborbital flight due to low speed following launch

Longer suborbital flight due to higher speed following launch

Orbital flight when object is given a speed of 28,000 kph (17,400 mph)

THRUST AND ACCELERATION ▶

A rocket burns fuel to produce a jet of hot, expanding gas. The action of the gas being blasted downwards causes a reaction force, or thrust, that pushes the rocket upwards. This provides a classic example of Newton's third law of motion, which states that every action has an equal and opposite reaction. The upward thrust on the rocket exceeds the force of gravity pulling the rocket towards the ground. There is therefore an overall upward force on the rocket that causes it to accelerate up through the atmosphere.

Thrust acts on a rocket to accelerate it upwards

Rocket propelled upwards, in reaction to explosive downward flow of its exhaust gases

rockets

Gravity acts downwards, towards Earth's centre

Solid-fuel boosters deliver more than 90 per cent of the total launch thrust

Main stage fuselage contains the rocket's fuel tanks

GRAVITY IN SPACE ▶

When astronauts float through space, it seems that gravity is no longer affecting them. In fact, the force of gravity on the astronaut is almost the same as the gravity acting on someone on Earth. The difference is that the astronaut is in a state called free-fall – falling without ever reaching the ground. An astronaut in free-fall is weightless. If he or she were to stand on some scales, they would show no weight, because the scales would be falling too.

Main engine burns for about 10 minutes on launch, varying slightly according to the mission

Fiery hot exhaust gases propel the rocket upwards

ROCKET HISTORY

The rockets that launch spacecraft today can trace their history back to Germany in the 1930s. People in other countries had been building small rockets and thinking about space travel for many years, but it was a team of scientists and engineers in Germany that led the world in rocket design. They eventually went on to build the most advanced rockets of the day, such as the V-2. Many of these scientists and engineers later developed rockets for the USA and Soviet Union, including the rockets that took astronauts to the Moon.

◀ ON PAPER
The great Soviet engineer Sergei Korolev sketched this rocket design during the 1940s. Korolev started building rockets in the 1930s. During the 1950s, he produced missiles used for military purposes. His R-5 missile, based on the design shown here, was first launched in 1953. Korolev went on to mastermind the Soviet Union's space programme, designing the rocket that launched the first satellite and the Vostok rocket that took Yuri Gagarin into orbit in 1961.

◀ AN EARLY START
The first liquid-fuelled rocket was launched in 1926 by the American Robert Goddard. During launch and flight, oxygen gas was produced at high pressure and used to force petrol and liquid oxygen along separate lines to the combustion chamber. Goddard's rocket climbed to a height of 12.5 m (41 ft) during a flight that lasted 2.5 seconds. Later liquid-fuelled rockets had the great advantage over solid-fuelled rockets that they could be turned on and off.

e ►► rockets

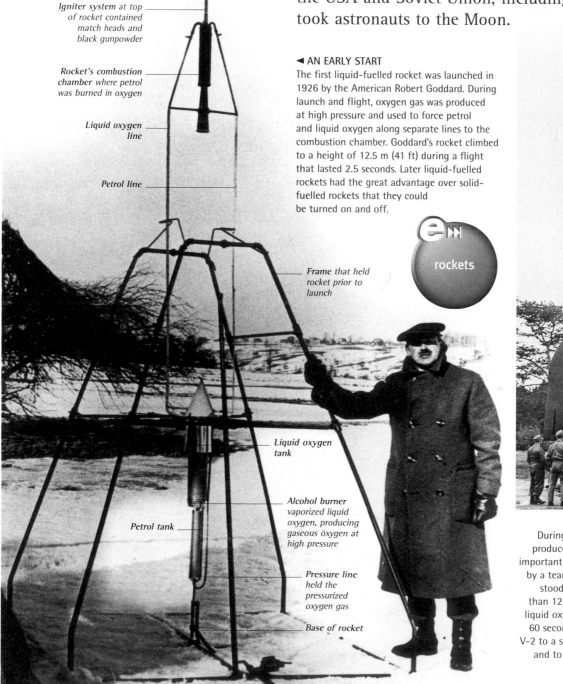

Igniter system at top of rocket contained match heads and black gunpowder

Rocket's combustion chamber where petrol was burned in oxygen

Liquid oxygen line

Petrol line

Frame that held rocket prior to launch

Liquid oxygen tank

Alcohol burner vaporized liquid oxygen, producing gaseous oxygen at high pressure

Petrol tank

Pressure line held the pressurized oxygen gas

Base of rocket

WAR ROCKET ▲
During World War II (1939-1945), Germany produced a series of new weapons. The most important was the V-2 rocket. It was developed by a team led by Wernher von Braun. The V-2 stood 14 m (50 ft) high and weighed more than 12 tonnes. It was fuelled by alcohol and liquid oxygen and its engine burned for about 60 seconds. In that short time, it boosted the V-2 to a speed of about 5,600 kph (3,500 mph) and to a height of nearly 100 km (62 miles).

This monument in Kaluga, Russia, honours Konstantin Tsiolkovsky, a Russian school-teacher who worked out many of the principles of rocketry more than 50 years before the Space Age began. Tsiolkovsky had been fascinated by the idea of space travel since his childhood and started writing about space flight in 1898. He could not afford to build and test his own rockets, so most of his work was in the form of theories and calculations on paper.

Escape system propelled the command module to safety in the event of a launch failure

Command module housed the three astronauts for most of their journey

Service module contained fuel, a rocket motor, and oxygen for the astronauts

Housing for the lunar module, which took two astronauts to the Moon's surface

Third stage fired to place Apollo in Earth orbit, then re-ignited to send it to the Moon

▲ LAUNCHING A SATELLITE
The Jupiter C rocket launched the first US satellite in 1958. When used to launch satellites, the rocket was known as Juno I. It was developed by Wernher von Braun and members of his V-2 rocket team, who had moved to the USA at the end of World War II. The Jupiter C was developed from designs for the Redstone rocket, which went on to launch the first two American astronauts in 1961.

ROCKET TO THE MOON ►
Saturn V, the giant rocket that sent US astronauts to the Moon, was developed at NASA's Marshall Space Flight Center under the leadership of Wernher von Braun. With an Apollo spacecraft on top of its three stages, it stood 111 m (363 ft) high and weighed 3,000 tonnes. It could launch a spacecraft weighing 152 tonnes into Earth orbit or send a 53-tonne spacecraft to the Moon. After the Apollo missions ended, a two-stage version of Saturn V launched the Skylab space station in 1973.

ROCKET POWER

It takes an enormous amount of energy to boost a spacecraft into orbit. Rockets powered by explosive chemical reactions are still the only vehicles capable of getting to space. A rocket is propelled by a jet of gas produced by burning fuel. Oxygen is needed to burn the fuel. Since there is no oxygen in space, rockets carry their own supply. The largest launchers are actually two or more rockets, called stages, on top of each other. As each stage uses up its fuel, it falls away to save weight.

FOUR STEPS TO ORBIT

LIFT- OFF
During lift-off, Ariane 5's main engine fires first, followed 7 seconds later by its solid fuel boosters. Two minutes later, the boosters separate. In that short time, each has burned 238 tonnes of fuel. The boosters fall away when the rocket has reached a height of about 65 km (40 miles) and a speed of about 7,450 kph (4,620 mph).

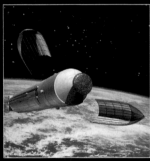

FAIRING JETTISONED
Just over 3 minutes after lift-off, the rocket is more than 100 km (62 miles) above the ground. It has passed through the thickest part of the atmosphere, so the streamlined fairing around the payload is no longer needed. It splits in two and falls away. Different fairings are used depending on the size and shape of the payload that has to fit inside.

STAGE SEPARATION
Ariane 5's first or main stage engine is shut down about 9 minutes 42 seconds after lift-off. The rocket is now at a height of 150 km (93 miles) and travelling at 28,000 kph (17,400 mph). A few seconds later, the first stage separates from the rest of the rocket. As it falls back through the atmosphere, it breaks up and falls into the Pacific Ocean.

SECOND STAGE IGNITES
Finally, Ariane 5's second or upper stage engine fires to boost the payload into the correct orbit. The second stage engine can burn for up to about 18 minutes. The precise burn time depends on the type and height of orbit into which the payload is to be placed. Once the payload has been released, Ariane 5 has completed its work.

ARIANE 5 ▶
An Ariane 5 rocket blasts off from the European Space Agency's spaceport in French Guiana, South America. The 750-tonne rocket's first flight was in June 1996 and it first successfully launched a commercial satellite into space in December 1999. It can launch satellites weighing up to 8,000 kg (17,600 lb).

Payload fairing splits in two to release payload

Payload can include two large satellites and several small microsatellites

Second stage engine boosts the payload into its final orbit

Solid fuel booster supplies extra power for take-off

Hydrogen tank contains 25 tonnes of liquid hydrogen; at the top is the liquid oxygen tank

Solid rocket boosters hold 238 tonnes of solid propellant and burn for 130 seconds

Exhaust nozzle of first, main stage engine can be swivelled to steer the rocket

Exhaust flame of solid-fuel booster rocket

esa

cnes

SPACECRAFT MANOEUVRING

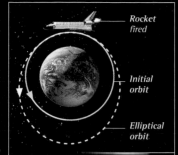

FORWARD THRUST
Firing a rocket to speed up a spacecraft in the direction it is already moving pushes it further away from Earth into an elliptical orbit. In this orbit, the spacecraft speeds up as it comes closer to Earth and slows down as it travels further away. If the rocket is fired when the craft is at its furthest point from Earth, the orbit will become circular.

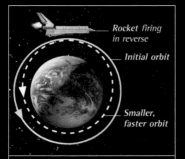

REVERSE THRUST
Turning round and firing a rocket in the direction a spacecraft is moving slows the craft down. Gravity then pulls it down into a lower orbit. As it falls, it speeds up. The closer to Earth it gets, the faster the craft must go to resist gravity and stay in orbit. If reverse thrust is used for long enough, gravity wins and the craft returns to Earth.

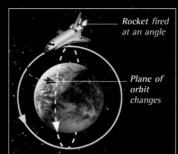

CHANGING THE ORBITAL PLANE
To change the plane of its orbit, a spacecraft must fire a rocket at an angle to its direction of motion. This may sound simple, but working out exactly how long to fire the rocket for and in which direction is quite complicated. Spacecraft rarely change their orbital plane, because it uses up large amounts of fuel.

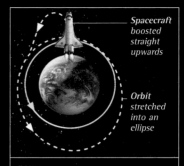

RADIAL THRUST
Firing a rocket straight away from Earth usually has a similar result to a forward thrust. Unless the rocket burns long and powerfully enough to cause the spacecraft to completely escape Earth's gravity, the spacecraft eventually falls back towards Earth again. As it does so, the spacecraft speeds up and its circular orbit becomes elliptical.

STEERING ROCKETS ▶
As a rocket soars away from the launch-pad, control systems on board monitor its direction of motion and make many tiny adjustments to keep it on a stable flight path. They steer the rocket in the right direction by swivelling its engine nozzle. Swivelling the nozzle like this is called gimballing. A gimballed nozzle doesn't have to move much. A rocket travels so fast and so far that it can be kept on course by very small adjustments to its direction of motion.

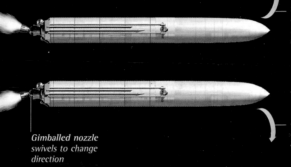

Rocket swings in opposite direction to nozzle orientation

Gimballed nozzle swivels to change direction

Rocket swings round and flies in a new direction

 rockets

TESTING ROCKETS ▲
New rocket engines are test-fired on the ground to make sure that they work and to measure precisely how powerful they are. They have to be held down securely in test-stands to stop them from moving. Successful rockets are continually improved and tested again and again. The Vulcan engine that powers the first stage of the Ariane 5 rocket was test-fired about 300 times during its development.

Fiery jet is sent along the ground as the rocket is test-fired sideways

Instruments measure the rocket's exhaust

Exhaust nozzle of engine being tested

◄ **SPUTNIK 1**
Sputnik's full name was Iskustvennyi Sputnik Zemli, ("Fellow Traveller of Earth"). Sputnik 1 was a metal ball with four radio aerials sticking out of it, each about 3 m (10 ft) long. It was launched by a modified R-7 military rocket. When it passed overhead, every 96 minutes, its bleep radio signal could be picked up on the ground below. After three weeks, its batteries were exhausted and it fell silent. On 4 January 1958, after 1,400 orbits, it re-entered Earth's atmosphere and burned up.

FIRST SATELLITES

The Space Age began on 4 October 1957, when the Soviet Union launched Sputnik 1, the first artificial satellite. Early satellites were small, simple, and powered by batteries, which lasted for only a few weeks. At first, just getting a satellite into orbit was an achievement, because rockets were so unreliable. If they didn't go off course or explode, upper stages sometimes failed to fire. Many early satellites were blown to bits or crashed back to Earth a few minutes after lift-off.

Thin outer shell was highly polished to reflect heat radiation

Inner shell was filled with nitrogen gas

Two small radio transmitters fitted under the inner shell

"The assault on space has begun"

Sergei Korolev, Russian rocket scientist

◄ **EARLY SPACE STUDIES**
The first US satellite, Explorer 1, was launched on 31 January 1958. It carried instruments to study cosmic rays (tiny particles whizzing through space) and discovered the Van Allen radiation belts – a doughnut-shaped region around Earth filled with charged particles trapped by Earth's magnetic field. Its radio transmissions stopped in May 1958, but it stayed in space for another 12 years and made 58,000 orbits before burning up in the atmosphere.

BUILDING SPUTNIK ►
Sputnik 1 was made from an alloy of aluminium, the same material used to make aircraft. Aluminium was chosen because it is lightweight, inexpensive, and easily shaped. The Soviet space programme's chief designer, Sergei Korolev, stood at the shoulders of the metal-workers and engineers while they made and fitted each part. Sputnik 1 was built from standard parts inside a simple casing.

Zinc batteries provided power to the two radio transmitters

Thermometer monitored temperature as Sputnik reached altitudes as high as 946 km (588 miles)

◄ **BAD NEWS**
America's first attempt to put a satellite in orbit had been a failure. The Vanguard satellite was due to launch on 6 December 1957, two months after Sputnik 1. When the countdown reached zero, the rocket fired. It rose just 1 m (3 ft) off the launch-pad, then fell back and exploded. Some newspapers nicknamed the satellite Dudnik or Kaputnik. Within two months the US successfully launched Explorer 1.

satellites

DECADES IN SPACE ►

The first Vanguard satellite went into space on 17 March 1958, and is still orbiting Earth. It is a small sphere with two radio transmitters inside, though these no longer work. One was powered by a battery and the other by six solar cells stuck on the satellite's body. The radios transmitted by means of six aerials. It also contains two sensors, called thermistors, which measured the temperature inside the satellite.

Radio aerials were 30 cm (12 in) long

Satellite body was made in two halves, joined by a ring around the middle

SATELLITE TELEVISION ►

Telstar was the first of a new type of communications satellite. Satellites had relayed radio signals before, but the signals bounced off them like light off a mirror. Telstar received signals and then re-transmitted them. It could relay signals across the Atlantic Ocean for 20 minutes per orbit. It relayed the first live transatlantic television pictures and the first telephone call to travel through space on 23 July 1962. Telstar caught the public imagination – a British pop group (the Tornadoes) even had a hit with a tune called *Telstar*.

SCIENTIFIC SUCCESS ▲

Explorer 6 was a small scientific research satellite launched on 7 August 1959, to study radiation, cosmic rays, Earth's magnetism, and micrometeorites. It was also equipped with a TV camera. Electric power was supplied by four solar panels sticking out from the satellite like waterwheel paddles. Although one of these failed to unfold properly, the others supplied enough power to operate the camera. It sent back the first pictures of Earth from space.

Live TV pictures were first relayed across the Atlantic by Telstar

Receiving aerial received radio signals from Earth

Solar cells generated electricity from sunlight

WATCHING THE WEATHER ►

TIROS 1 was the first weather satellite. TIROS stood for Television and Infra-Red Observation Satellite. It was launched on 1 April 1960. Each of the satellite's two television cameras could take 16 pictures on each Earth orbit. Two tape recorders stored up to 48 pictures until the satellite passed over a ground station that could receive them. By the time its batteries ran out, after 78 days, it had transmitted 22,952 pictures of Earth's weather.

Transmitting aerials sent weather pictures to Earth

Shuttle's robot arm
pushes the satellite away
from the Shuttle

◄ PUTTING A SATELLITE IN ORBIT
This satellite, called a Spartan 201, is designed to study the Sun's
corona (outer layer). Here it has just been lifted out of the Space
Shuttle's payload bay. When the arm lets go, the satellite
doesn't fall back to Earth, but stays close by. That is because
the Shuttle has already boosted it to orbital speed. Most
satellites orbit further from Earth than the Space Shuttle
does, so satellites launched by the Shuttle have a small
rocket attached to them to boost them to a higher orbit.

Instrument carrier
contains equipment to
study the Sun's corona

Service module
contains data recorders,
an altitude control
system, and electronics

VARIOUS EARTH ORBITS ►
Satellites and other spacecraft can
orbit around Earth's equator or from pole
to pole, or at any angle in between. They can
orbit close to Earth or further away. The orbit may
be circular or stretched into an ellipse. A spacecraft's
orbit is chosen according to what it has been put in
space to do. For example, some satellites are put into a
special orbit at a fixed height above the equator, called
a geostationary orbit. A satellite in a geostationary orbit
goes round Earth in exactly the same time it takes
Earth to spin once on its own axis, which means the
satellite always sits above a particular point on
the equator. This can be a very useful orbit
for communications satellites.

ORBITS

When a spacecraft's speed is boosted to about 28,000 kph
(17,400 mph), Earth's gravity can no longer pull it back
down to the ground. Instead, gravity combines with the
spacecraft's speed to cause the craft to follow a curved path
around the planet. The endless path of a spacecraft or
moon around a planet is called an orbit and can be shaped
either like a circle or an ellipse (a stretched circle). The speed
of an orbiting craft depends on how far it is from the planet.
The closer it is, the faster it has to fly
to balance the pull of gravity.

Geostationary orbit is a
circular orbit at a height of
35,800 km (22,250 miles)
above the equator and in
the same direction as Earth
spins on its own axis

Antenna dish is kept
facing in one direction
while other parts of
the satellite spin

THE PHYSICS OF ORBITS

If you are whirled around by a
fairground ride, your body tries
to fly outwards, but the seat or
outside wall of the ride holds you
in place by exerting a force
towards the ride's centre.
Similarly, a ball whirled in
a circle on a piece of string is
constantly pulled towards the
centre by tension in the string.

A spacecraft orbiting a planet
behaves in a similar way. The
planet's gravity stops the craft
from flying away by pulling it
towards the centre of the planet
and curling its
path into
a curve.

If the force is removed,
the ball carries on in the
same direction

String under
tension pulls
ball towards
centre

Force towards
centre pulls ball
around in a circle

orbits

Solar panel generates
electricity as sunlight
falls on it

Equipment is designed
to fit into the satellite's
cylindrical shape

Wheel riders are
moved in a circle
by a constant
force directed
towards the
centre of the
wheel as it spins

Thruster
corrects spin if
sensors in the
satellite detect
a wobble

Cylindrical shape
is typical for a
spin-stabilized
satellite

◄ SPIN-STABILIZED SATELLITE
Satellites must be kept steady in space so that
their antennae, cameras, or other instruments
are kept pointing in the right direction.
One way of stabilizing a satellite is to make
use of a basic principle of physics called the
gyroscopic principle. This states that if an
object is made to spin, it resists any change
to the direction in which it is pointing.
A spin-stabilized satellite, like this HS 376
communications satellite, is kept pointing
in one direction by making the main part
of the satellite spin. Only its antennae and
equipment like cameras is not made to spin.

THREE-AXIS STABILIZED SATELLITE ▶
Some satellites, such as this advanced communications satellite called Artemis, are kept steady in space by a method called three-axis stabilization. Small thrusters turn the satellite until it points in the right direction. These thrusters can rotate the satellite around any of three directions, or axes, at right angles to one another. If the satellite starts turning out of position, the thrusters automatically fire and bring it back again.

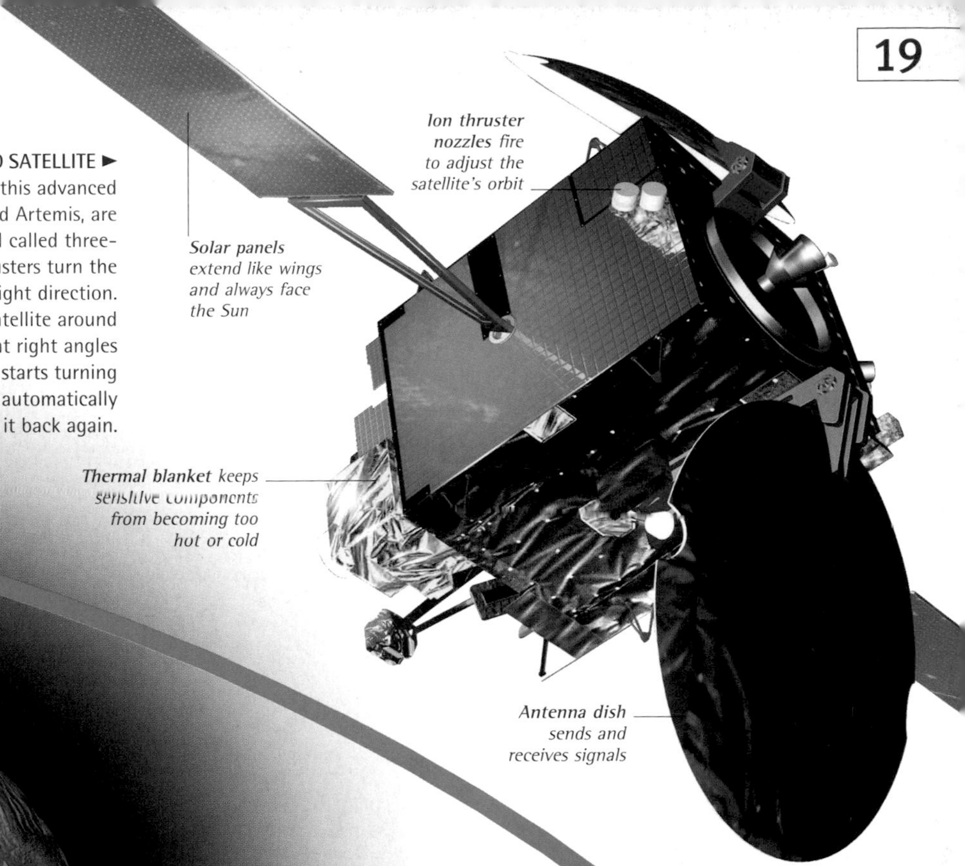

Ion thruster nozzles fire to adjust the satellite's orbit

Solar panels extend like wings and always face the Sun

Thermal blanket keeps sensitive components from becoming too hot or cold

Antenna dish sends and receives signals

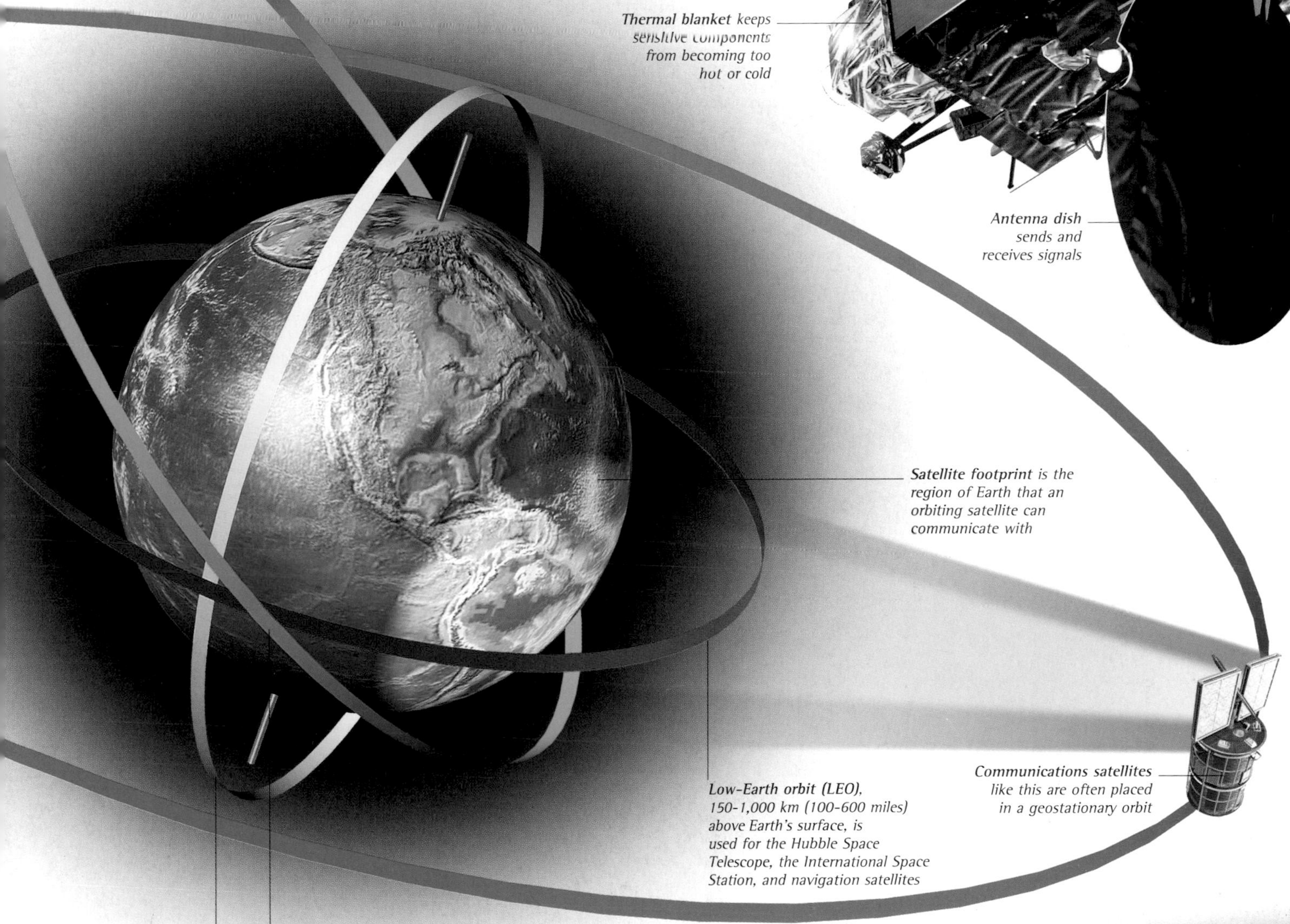

Satellite footprint is the region of Earth that an orbiting satellite can communicate with

Communications satellites like this are often placed in a geostationary orbit

Low-Earth orbit (LEO), 150-1,000 km (100-600 miles) above Earth's surface, is used for the Hubble Space Telescope, the International Space Station, and navigation satellites

Polar orbit goes over Earth's poles, usually at a height of about 800 km (500 miles), and is often used for Earth-monitoring satellites

Elliptical orbit varies from hundreds to many thousands of kilometres in height and is used for some scientific and communications satellites

FORMATION FLYING ▶
Most satellites spend their whole working lives orbiting Earth on their own, but the Cluster II project is different. Four identical satellites were launched in 2000 and orbit together in close formation. Their elliptical orbit varies from 19,000 km to 119,000 km (11,200 to 74,000 miles) above Earth's surface. The instruments on board take simultaneous measurements and so give a three-dimensional picture of the changes that are happening in the space around Earth.

FIRST SPACE PROBES

The first space probes to visit other worlds were aimed at our closest neighbour in space, the Moon. To break away from Earth orbit and head into space, they had to be boosted to a speed of 40,000 kph (24,850 mph). Once the race to land the first astronauts on the Moon was under way, the USA and Soviet Union sent dozens of probes to study and photograph the Moon in great detail. Space probes flew past the Moon, crashed into it, orbited it, and made controlled landings on its surface.

Hinged panel was one of four that opened up like flower petals

Radio aerial transmitted data from on-board instruments

Metal sphere contained scientific instruments and a radio transmitter

Television camera took the first photographs on the Moon's surface

Rod aerial was one of four that transmitted pictures to Earth

▲ LUNA 9 CAPSULE
Luna 9 was the first spacecraft to make a controlled, or soft, landing on the Moon. It landed in a region of the Moon called the Ocean of Storms, on 3 February 1966. As it touched the surface, it ejected an egg-shaped capsule, 60 cm (24 in) long and weighing 100 kg (220 lb). When the capsule came to rest, it opened to reveal a camera and radio aerials. They enabled Luna 9 to send the first pictures from the Moon's surface.

▲ LUNA 1
The Soviet probe Luna 1 was the first spacecraft to escape from Earth and go into space. The spherical craft, launched on 2 January 1959, was meant to hit the Moon but missed and became the first spacecraft to go into orbit around the Sun. Luna 3, launched on 7 October 1959, took the first photographs of the far side of the Moon.

probes

Spacecraft stood 3.1 m (10 ft) high and weighed 366 kg (807 lb)

TV cameras gave two wide-angle and four narrow-angle views

Television system and omnidirectional radio antennae

RANGER 9 COLLISION COURSE

TARGET MOON
Ranger 9 was the last of the Ranger craft. It was launched on 21 March 1965. Just over 64 hours later, at a distance of 2,261 km (1,404 miles) from the Moon, its cameras were switched on and it began transmitting pictures.

CLOSING IN
Ranger 9's pictures showed it had drifted 4.8 km (3 miles) off course after a flight of 417,054 km (259,145 miles). It was heading into the middle of a crater called Alphonsus, close to the centre of the Moon's near side.

CRASH!
Ranger 9's cameras took 5,814 photographs in the last 14 minutes of its flight. The final frames showed rocks and craters as small as 30 cm (1 ft) across. Then the probe crashed into the surface at 9,617 kph (5,975 mph).

RANGER 9 MOON-PROBE ▲
The US Ranger probes were designed to take close-up photographs of the Moon. The photographs were needed to find suitable landing sites for later, manned missions. The probes were deliberately crashed into the Moon, sending back pictures all the way. The pictures showed 1,000 times more detail than could be seen by telescopes on Earth. Rangers 1-6 failed, but Rangers 7-9 were successful and sent back more than 17,000 photographs.

Dark areas, or
maria, are regions
where lava flowed
in the distant past

Craters were caused
by rocks of different
sizes crashing onto
the surface

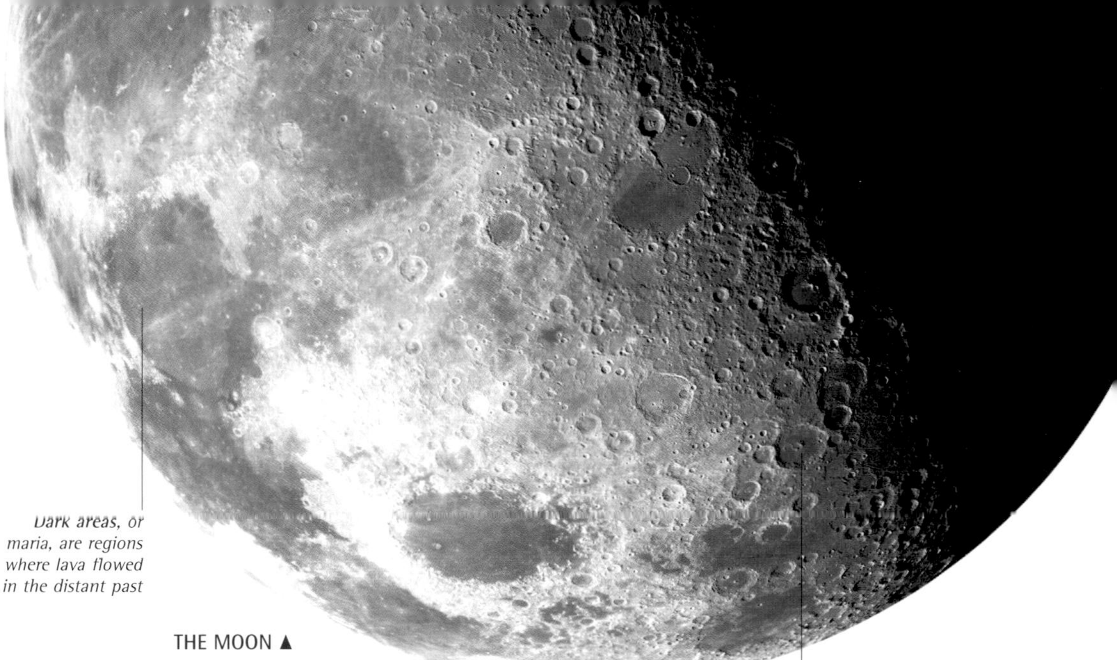

THE MOON ▲
The Moon has been accompanying Earth
on its travels around the Sun for four and
a half billion years. It orbits Earth at an average
distance of 384,000 km (238,000 miles). The
dark parts on its surface are called maria,
meaning seas, but they contain no water. The
brighter parts are highland areas.

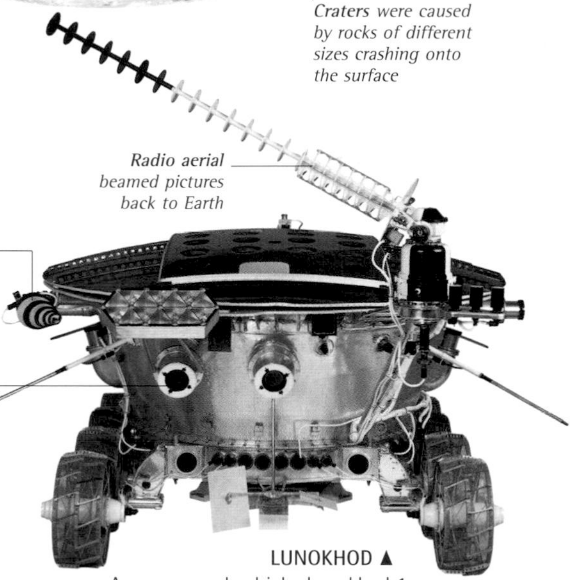

▲ LUNAR ORBITER BLAST-OFF
The first US Lunar Orbiter probe took off for
the Moon on 10 August 1966. After the Ranger
probes, Lunar Orbiter was the second of three
US unmanned projects leading up to manned
Moon-landings. The Lunar Orbiters took
photographs of the Moon and made precise
measurements of its gravity. Five Orbiter probes
were sent to the Moon in 1966 and 1967, and
all five were successful.

Radio aerial
beamed pictures
back to Earth

Omnidirectional
antenna received
radio signals from
Earth that steered
the rover

Television camera
showed the driver on
Earth the view ahead

LUNOKHOD ▲
An unmanned vehicle, Lunokhod 1,
landed in the Moon's Sea of Rains in 1970.
A driver on Earth steered it around, guided by
its cameras. Lunokhod 1 spent nearly a year
studying lunar soil and rocks. Lunokhod 2
landed in the Sea of Serenity in 1973.
It travelled three times as far and managed
to climb a 400-m (1,300-ft) mountain.

Solar panels
produce electricity
from sunlight

Television camera
can swivel around
360 degrees

Mast holds solar
panels above
the probe

SURVEYOR 3 ►
Surveyor 3 landed in the
Moon's Ocean of Storms
on 20 April 1967. It took 6,317
photographs and dug a trench
in the surface. Surveyor was
the third US unmanned
Moon project. Each Surveyor
spacecraft was designed
to make a controlled landing
on the Moon and test the
firmness of its surface. In
November 1969, Apollo
12's lunar module landed
close to Surveyor 3. The
Apollo astronauts returned
parts of the probe to Earth,
where scientists studied how
its stay on the Moon had
affected them.

EARLY MANNED CRAFT

The first manned spacecraft were also called capsules: they were small and extremely cramped. Each type was built to achieve a specific objective. The US Mercury and Soviet Vostok capsules were designed to get one person into space and back to Earth again. They could keep an astronaut or cosmonaut alive in space for about a day. The next generation of Soviet spacecraft, called Voskhod, could carry more than one person, while the US Gemini spacecraft were designed to carry two astronauts on longer spaceflights, lasting up to about a fortnight.

Storage compartment contained parachutes for landing

Corrugations strengthened the capsule

Astronaut entered through a hatch in the wall

MERCURY SPECIFICATIONS

Height: 2.92 m (9.6 ft)
Base diameter: 1.89 m (6.2 ft)
Mass: 1,935 kg (4,265 lb)
Crew: One
Launch rocket: Redstone (suborbital flights) Atlas (orbital flights)
Manned missions: Two suborbital missions Four orbital missions
Longest mission: 1 day 10 hours 20 minutes by Mercury 9 (22 Earth orbits)
Landing method: After re-entry, the capsule parachuted into the ocean with the astronaut on board

◄ MERCURY CAPSULE
The Mercury capsule was made from titanium, a strong but light metal. It contained an atmosphere of pure oxygen, sealed inside an inner hull. In space, the astronaut could turn the capsule around by firing small thrusters. Three solid-fuel rockets were fired to slow the capsule down and begin re-entry. A heat shield covered the broad end of the capsule to protect it during re-entry.

Heat shield protected capsule on re-entry

Radio antenna for communications with Earth

Re-entry capsule was the part that detached and returned to Earth

Spherical tanks held oxygen and nitrogen for life support

Instrument module contained instruments for controlling orbital flight

◄ VOSTOK SPACECRAFT
Vostok's re-entry capsule, where the cosmonaut sat, was a steel sphere covered with heat shield material. It contained life support equipment, TV and film cameras, a radio system, control panels, food, and water. Four metal straps attached it to an instrument module. The re-entry capsule separated from the instrument module just before it.re-entered Earth's atmosphere.

first astronauts

VOSTOK SPECIFICATIONS

Height: 7.35 m (24.2 ft)
Diameter: 2.50 m (8.2 ft)
Mass: 4,725 kg (10,416 lb)
Crew: One
Launch rocket: Vostok 8K72K (also called A-1)
Manned missions: Six orbital missions
Longest mission: 4 days 23 hours 6 minutes by Vostok 5 (81 Earth orbits)
Landing method: Soon after re-entry, an ejection seat in the capsule fired, and the cosmonaut parachuted to the ground

INSIDE VOSKHOD ▲

To fit three people inside the Voskhod capsule, the ejection seat and other gear that had been fitted to Vostok were removed. It was still very cramped, so the crew did not wear spacesuits for the launch and landing. Voskhod 2 also carried a device called an airlock, which allowed one of its crew to make the first spacewalk.

VOSKHOD SPECIFICATIONS

Height: 5 m (16.45 ft)	
Diameter: 2.43 m (8 ft)	
Mass: Up to 5,682 kg (12,526 lb)	
Crew: Two or three	
Launch rocket: Voskhod 11A57 (also called A-2)	
Manned missions: Two orbital missions	
Longest mission: 1 day 2 hours 2 minutes by Voskhod 2 (17 orbits)	
Landing method: Capsule parachuted to the ground with the crew on board	

▲ VOSKHOD CAPSULE

The Soviet Union launched two manned missions between the last Vostok mission and the start of the Soyuz programme. They used a modified Vostok capsule, called Voskhod. The Voskhod spacecraft were the first to carry more than one person. Unlike Vostok, the Voskhod capsules landed by parachute with the crew still inside. When probes dangling from the parachute lines touched the ground, rockets fired to soften the landing.

GEMINI SPECIFICATIONS

Height: 5.61 m (18.5 ft)	
Base diameter: 3.05 m (10 ft)	
Mass: 3,760 kg (8,290 lb)	
Crew: Two	
Launch rocket: Titan	
Manned missions: Ten orbital missions	
Longest mission: 13 days 18 hours 35 minutes by Gemini 7 (206 Earth orbits)	
Landing method: Re-entry module parachuted into ocean with crew on board	

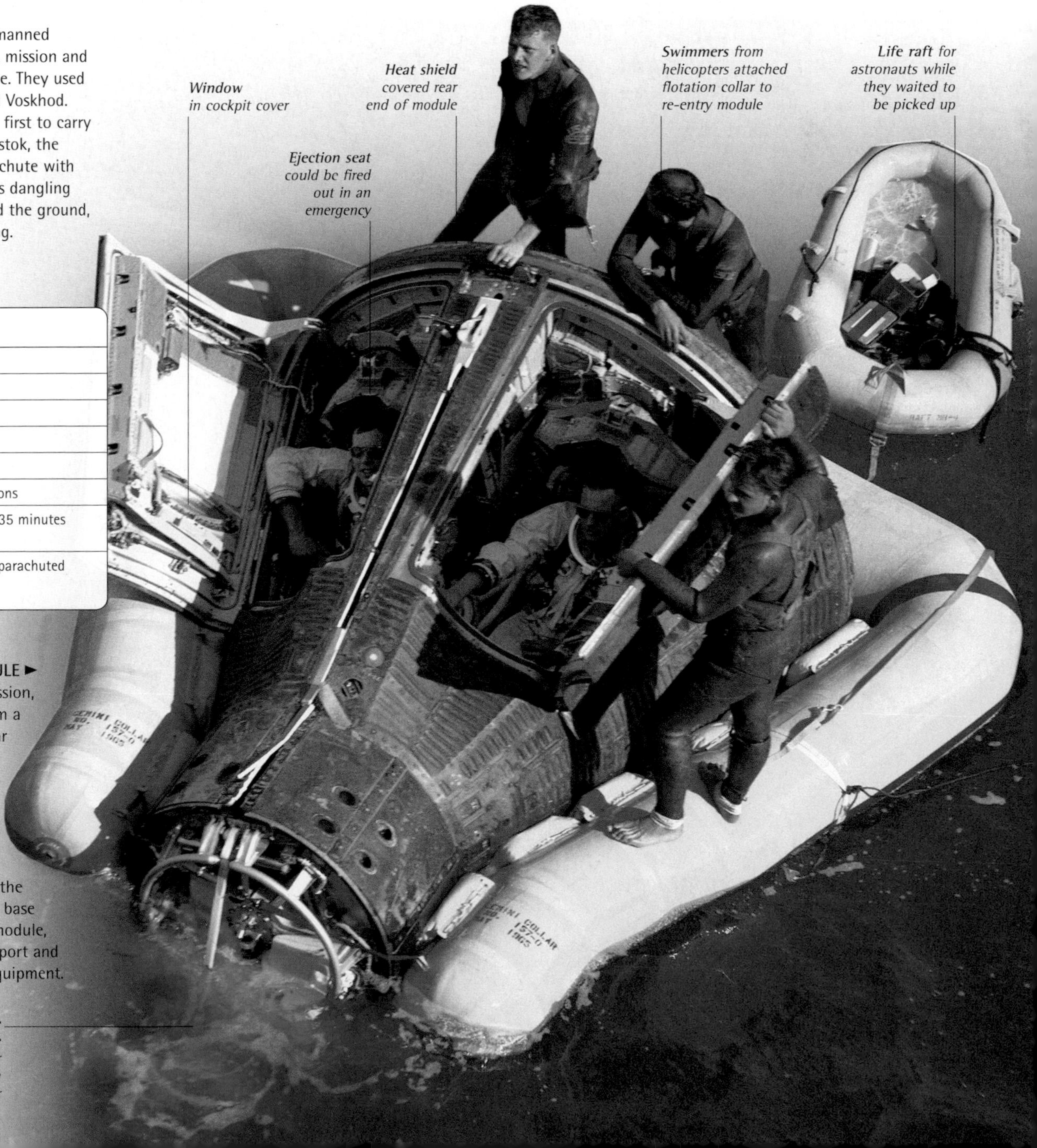

Window in cockpit cover

Heat shield covered rear end of module

Swimmers from helicopters attached flotation collar to re-entry module

Life raft for astronauts while they waited to be picked up

Ejection seat could be fired out in an emergency

GEMINI RE-ENTRY MODULE ►

At the end of a Gemini mission, swimmers would be dropped from a helicopter into the water near the re-entry module. They would attach a flotation device and then help the astronauts into a raft. The Gemini spacecraft had two parts, or modules. The re-entry module, shown here, carried the two astronauts. Attached to its base was a larger part, the adapter module, which contained life support and electrical equipment.

Green dye made the module easier to spot from the air

HUMANS IN SPACE

When the Soviet Union started launching animals into space in 1957, it was clear that a manned spaceflight was in preparation. Less than four years later, Yuri Gagarin became the first human in space. More soon followed – over the next 26 months, there were 12 US and Soviet manned flights. Soviet missions were shrouded in secrecy, but the US flights attracted huge attention. Two suborbital flights (ones not encircling Earth) by Alan Shepard and Gus Grissom were followed by four orbital flights by John Glenn, Scott Carpenter, Wally Schirra, and Gordon Cooper.

▲ GAGARIN
At 9:06 am Moscow time on 12 April 1961, Yuri Gagarin heard the rocket beneath his Vostok 1 capsule rumble and whine as it rose into the air. Nine minutes later, he was in orbit. As the capsule gently rotated, the blackness outside gave way to the brilliant blue Earth, then the Sun's blinding glare. He made one orbit of the Earth and then re-entered the atmosphere.

FRONT PAGE NEWS ▶
As a result of his historic flight, Gagarin was transformed overnight from being an unknown Soviet Air Force officer into the most famous person in the world. His face looked out from newspapers and everyone wanted to meet him. Wherever he went, crowds lined the roads to see him. In Britain, he was invited to lunch with the Queen.

Nikita Khruschev *Valentina Tereshkova* *Andrian Nikolayev* *Yuri Gagarin*

SOVIET SUCCESS ▶
The trio of cosmonauts shown here sharing a joke with Soviet Premier Nikita Khrushchev all flew in space. Andrian Nikolayev was the third cosmonaut (after Gagarin and Gherman Titov) to go into orbit, aboard Vostok 3 on 11 August 1962. He made 64 orbits in a flight that lasted nearly four days. Valentina Tereshkova became the first woman in space, on 6 June 1963.

◀ MERCURY 3 LAUNCH
On 5 May 1961, a Redstone rocket carried Alan Shepard into space on the first US manned space mission, Mercury 3. The rocket was not powerful enough to put Shepard's capsule, which was given the call sign Freedom 7, into orbit. It reached a height of 187 km (116 miles), then fell back to Earth, splashing down in the Atlantic 15 minutes after lift-off and 488 km (303 miles) from the launch site in Florida.

FIRST AMERICAN IN SPACE ▶
Alan Shepard was a navy test-pilot before joining NASA. After his successful Mercury flight, he was scheduled to fly in the first Gemini mission, but was grounded because of a problem with his inner ear. After surgery in 1969, he returned to flight. Less than 10 years after his Mercury mission, he stood on the Moon as commander of Apollo 14.

ANIMALS IN SPACE

The first space travellers were animals, not humans. Animals were sent first to see if it was possible to survive a spaceflight and to test the craft carrying them. The Soviet Union used mainly dogs, and the USA used chimpanzees.

DOGS

The first living creature to orbit Earth was a dog called Laika, travelling aboard the Sputnik 2 satellite on 3 November 1957. Several more test-flights were made with dogs to test the Vostok capsule.

CHIMPANZEE

Ham, a chimpanzee, was one of the most famous animals to travel into space aboard an early US space mission.

He was launched in a Mercury capsule on a suborbital flight on 31 January 1961.

MICE

Living creatures are still carried into space as the subjects of scientific experiments. The Space Shuttle carried some mice in 2001, to test a protein that may one day help astronauts resist bone loss during long missions.

SPIDERS

Skylab 3 carried two spiders, called Anita and Arabella. Scientists wanted to see if they could spin webs while weightless – they could. Spiders were carried again in the ill-fated last flight of the Space Shuttle Columbia.

Capsule on Glenn's flight was given the call sign Friendship 7

Window replaced two small portholes of earlier capsules

Hatch sealed by a cover held in place by 70 bolts

Glenn's flight capsule, Friendship 7

President Kennedy presents Glenn with his medal

▲ FIRST AMERICAN INTO ORBIT

On 20 February 1962, American astronaut John Glenn squeezed into his capsule for the Mercury 6 mission. At 9:47 am, flames erupted from its Atlas booster and Glenn soared into space. During the flight, an indicator showed that the capsule had a loose heat shield and might burn up during re-entry. Glenn was told not to jettison his retro-rockets, because their straps might hold the heat shield on. He landed safely – the heat shield was not loose after all.

◄ CELEBRATED AS A HERO

Three days after Glenn's flight, US President John F. Kennedy presented him with a Distinguished Service Medal to recognize his achievement. The ceremony took place at the Cape Canaveral launch site in Florida. A week later, on 1 March 1962, four million people turned out in New York City when Glenn arrived for celebrations and to address the United Nations.

first astronauts

> *"I believe this nation should commit itself to achieving the goal, before this decade is out, of landing a man on the Moon...."*
> President John F. Kennedy

KENNEDY COMMITS TO SPACE ▲
On 25 May 1961, American President John F. Kennedy made an historic speech to the US Congress. It committed America to a manned Moon landing by the end of the 1960s. It was an amazingly bold announcement, because at that time America had not even put an astronaut into Earth orbit. In his speech Kennedy said, "No single space project in this period will be more impressive to mankind, or more important for the long-range exploration of space."

THE RACE BEGINS

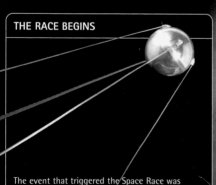

The event that triggered the Space Race was the launch of the first artificial satellite, Sputnik 1, on 4 October 1957. Sputnik 1 was just a small, harmless metal ball that bleeped as it passed overhead, but it worried Americans for two reasons. It showed that the Soviet Union was more advanced technologically than had previously been thought. It also showed that the Soviet Union had long-range rockets powerful enough to fly over US territory, spy on it, and perhaps even attack it with nuclear missiles.

SPACE RACE

The Soviet Union's early successes in space took the USA by surprise. In 1961, the newly elected American President, John F. Kennedy, considered what to do. Some advisers urged him to cancel the space programme, because the Soviets were already so far ahead. But Kennedy argued that American technology and industry should be able to match or overtake the Soviet Union. He challenged the Soviet Union to a head-on contest in space. Success was no longer a mere technical challenge, it was a matter of national pride. The Space Race was on, with both sides desperate to be the first to put a person on the Moon.

SOYUZ TAKES OFF ▶
After Vostok and Voskhod, the Soviet Union's next spacecraft was Soyuz. With Soyuz, the Soviet Union would make longer spaceflights, learn to manoeuvre in orbit, and dock with other craft. Meanwhile, a Moon-landing spacecraft and a giant rocket to launch it were being built in great secrecy. When the USA won the race to the Moon in 1969, Soviet Moon-landing plans were scrapped, and Soyuz became a ferry craft to transport cosmonauts to and from a series of space stations.

> *"Let the capitalist countries try to overtake us"*
> Premier Nikita Khrushchev

▲ KHRUSHCHEV IN CONTROL
Premier Nikita Khrushchev held power in the Soviet Union when the Space Age began. He was immensely proud that Soviet technology had beaten the USA, and that the world could see it. First, a Soviet satellite flew unchallenged over American territory. Then, in April 1961, Gagarin made his epic trip to space. Soviet firsts kept coming.

Space Race

GEMINI 7 IN ORBIT ►
This photograph of Gemini 7 was taken from Gemini 6 when the two spacecraft met up in Earth orbit. The Space Race really hotted up with the Gemini missions. Over the course of just 21 months in 1965-1966, the USA launched 10 two-man missions. Their aim was to learn how to do everything that would be necessary for a Moon-landing mission. Astronauts practised manoeuvring spacecraft, changing orbit, docking one craft with another, and walking in space. The Gemini 7 mission lasted 14 days – a record at that time.

Exhaust nozzle of main engine

Aft section contained a restartable rocket engine with a thrust of 71 kN (16,000 lbf)

Mid section contained propellant tanks

Radio antenna allowed the Agena to be controlled by Gemini craft

Forward section contained guidance systems and control electronics

Docking cone designed for Gemini craft to dock with

MISSION SEQUENCE	
USSR	*USA*
1961	
Vostok 1	
	Mercury 3
	Mercury 4
Vostok 2	
1962	
	Mercury 6
	Mercury 7
Vostok 3 + 4	
	Mercury 8
1963	
	Mercury 9
Vostok 5 + 6	
1964	
Voskhod 1	
1965	
Voskhod 2	
	Gemini 3
	Gemini 4
	Gemini 5
	Gemini 6 + 7
1966	
	Gemini 8
	Gemini 9
	Gemini 10
	Gemini 11
	Gemini 12
1967	
Soyuz 1	

▲ TARGET FOR GEMINI 8
US astronaut David Scott took this photograph of an Agena rocket hanging in space during the Gemini 8 mission. As he did so, his pilot Neil Armstrong inched the spacecraft towards the rocket and then docked with it. This was the first space docking. Their triumph nearly ended in disaster when a thruster (a small rocket engine) jammed on. It fired continuously and sent the two spacecraft into a dangerously fast spin. Armstrong undocked, turned off Gemini 8's main thrusters and switched to a back-up system to stop the spacecraft spinning.

COOPERATION AT LAST ►
American astronaut Donald (Deke) Slayton and Soviet cosmonaut Alexei Leonov posed for photographs during the Apollo-Soyuz Project in 1975. After the Moon landings, which marked the end of the Space Race, the USA and Soviet Union began cooperating in space. During this joint US-Soviet mission, an Apollo spacecraft docked with a Soyuz spacecraft. The crews visited each other's craft and carried out joint experiments. Slayton had been one of the first seven Americans selected for astronaut training in 1959, but this was his first trip into space.

APOLLO PROGRAMME

The final US manned space project in the race to the Moon was Apollo. The Apollo spacecraft was composed of three parts, or modules, launched by the giant Saturn V rocket. The tiny command module provided living quarters for the three-man crew. For most of the mission, it was attached to the service module, containing propulsion, electrical power, and life support systems. On Moon-landing missions, two astronauts would descend to the Moon's surface in the spider-like lunar module, while the third orbited the Moon in the command module.

Command module would contain three astronauts on manned flights

Adapter was designed to contain a lunar module

Third stage put spacecraft in orbit and sent it to the Moon on lunar missions

Second stage boosted vehicle to a height of 185 km (115 miles)

◄ APOLLO 4 LIFT-OFF
A Saturn V rocket rose from the launch pad for the first time at the start of the unmanned Apollo 4 mission on 9 November 1967. At 8.9 seconds before launch, the rocket's first stage engines started. Six seconds later, a deafening roar reached the spectators. As the countdown reached zero, computers released the rocket and it slowly climbed away into orbit 185 km (115 miles) above Earth. There, the third stage fired and pushed the Apollo spacecraft even higher. The flight was a great success.

First stage separated from rest of rocket about 150 seconds after lift-off

First stage engines, fuelled by kerosene and liquid oxygen, boosted vehicle to a height of 60 km (37 miles)

Apollo

Adapter doors opened to release lunar module

Adapter could split in four to open

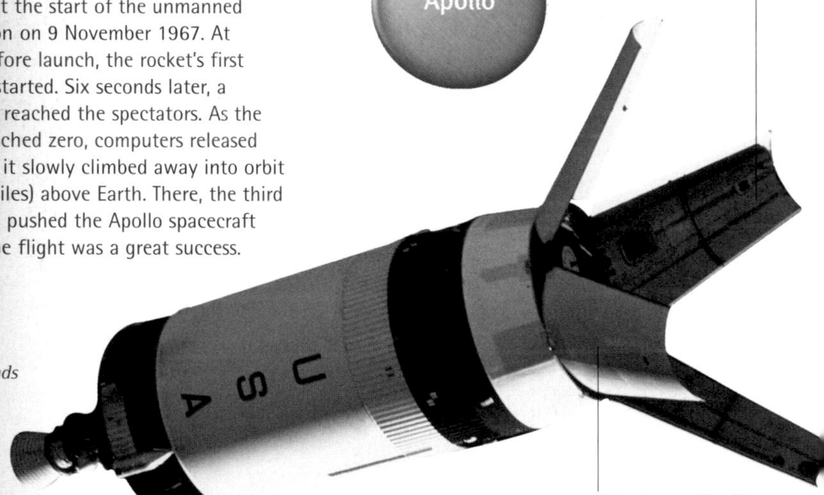

▲ APOLLO 7
The third stage of the Saturn V rocket used in the Apollo 7 mission is seen here with its attached adapter doors open. At the start of a Moon-landing mission, the adapter would house a lunar module. Apollo 7's adapter was empty. Even so, the crew put the spacecraft through all manoeuvres necessary to extract a lunar module from it. The Apollo 7 mission lasted nearly 11 days and was a success, although the three crew members developed severe colds in space.

APOLLO–SATURN V SPECIFICATIONS
APOLLO SPACECRAFT
Command module (CM) Length: 3.5 m (11 ft) Mass: 5.8 tonnes
Service module (SM) Length: 7.6 m (25 ft) Mass: 24.5 tonnes
Lunar module (LM) Length: 6.4 m (21 ft) Mass: 15 tonnes
SATURN V ROCKET
First stage (S–IC) Height: 42 m (138 ft) Mass: 2,287 tonnes
Second stage (S–II) Height: 25 m (82 ft) Mass: 488 tonnes
Third stage (S–IVB) Height: 18 m (59 ft) Mass: 119 tonnes
Apollo–Saturn V Height: 111 m (365 ft) Mass: 3,000 tonnes

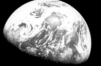

HEADING FOR THE MOON

A series of unmanned and manned Apollo missions led up to the first Moon-landing.

APOLLO 1

During a ground test of the new Apollo spacecraft on 27 January 1967, a fire broke out, killing the crew of Virgil (Gus) Grissom, Ed White, and Roger Chaffee. The spacecraft was later named Apollo 1.

APOLLO 2, 3

After the Apollo 1 fire, project plans changed. No missions were called Apollo 2 or 3.

APOLLO 4

On 9 November 1967, the Saturn V rocket made its first successful test-flight with an unmanned Apollo spacecraft.

APOLLO 5

On 22 January 1968, an Apollo lunar module was given its first unmanned test-flight in space.

APOLLO 6

On 4 April 1968, a Saturn V launched an Apollo spacecraft for a final unmanned test.

APOLLO 7

Launched on 11 October 1968, the manned Apollo 7 mission tested Apollo in Earth orbit.

APOLLO 8

Launched on 21 December 1968, Apollo 8 was the first manned flight to the Moon, which it orbited 10 times.

APOLLO 9

Launched on 3 March 1969, the manned Apollo 9 mission tested the lunar module in Earth orbit.

APOLLO 10

Launched on 18 May 1969, Apollo 10 was a dress rehearsal for the first Moon-landing. The lunar module was taken down almost to the Moon's surface.

EARTH RISE FROM APOLLO 8 ▲

This stunning view of Earth rising above the Moon's horizon was photographed by Frank Borman from the command module of Apollo 8, the first manned spacecraft to orbit the Moon. Borman, James Lovell, and Bill Anders made 10 Moon orbits on 24 and 25 December 1968 and transmitted the first live television pictures of the surface. After that, the only piece of Apollo hardware to test was the lunar module.

◄ DRESS REHEARSAL

This photograph of Apollo 10's command and service module (CSM) was taken by a crew member in the lunar module (LM). The Apollo 10 mission rehearsed everything for a Moon landing except the landing itself. Once the craft was in lunar orbit, two astronauts took the LM to within 14.5 km (9 miles) of the Moon's surface. The LM's top, ascent stage then separated from the descent stage and climbed to meet the CSM for the return flight to Earth.

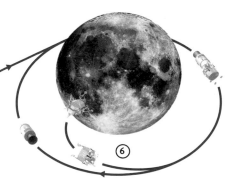

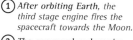

Discarded third stage

Lunar module

Command and service module

(1) After orbiting Earth, the third stage engine fires the spacecraft towards the Moon.

(2) The command and service module (CSM) separates from the third stage and turns around.

(3) Facing the opposite direction, the CSM docks with the lunar module, which is housed in the third stage.

(4) The CSM and attached lunar module turn around. The third stage is discarded.

(5) The spacecraft manoeuvres into lunar orbit.

(6) The lunar module separates from the CSM and lands on the Moon.

▲ LANDING ON THE MOON

The Apollo spacecraft had to perform a complex series of manoeuvres to achieve a Moon landing. It had to be turned and steered with great precision. Fine control of position and speed was essential for docking the command and service module (CSM) with the lunar module. The crew controlled the spacecraft by firing small thrusters arranged around the service module and lunar module. The service module's main engine was used for manoeuvres that needed more power, such as entering and leaving lunar orbit.

APOLLO 11 – MOONWALK

On the morning of 16 July 1969, nearly a million people gathered around the Kennedy Space Center to see history being made. Hundreds of millions more people all over the world, one fifth of Earth's population, watched the events unfold live on television. At 9:32 am local time, a deafening roar erupted from launch-pad 39A and Apollo 11 climbed into a clear blue sky, carrying the first explorers in history to travel to another world. Four days later, first Neil Armstrong and then Edwin (Buzz) Aldrin stepped onto the surface of the Moon.

Aldrin, suit, and backpack weigh 27 kg (60 lb) on the Moon, one sixth of their weight on Earth

Neil Armstrong and the lunar module are reflected in Aldrin's gold-coated visor

Control unit allows Aldrin to adjust his life support and communications systems

Multilayered suit composed mainly of tough artificial fibres

◄ NEIL ARMSTRONG'S FOOTPRINT
Neil Armstrong made the first human footprint on the Moon as he stepped off the lunar module's footpad onto the surface. The fine grey dust recorded his foot-fall perfectly. Without wind or rain to wear it away, it could still be there 10 million years from now. Eventually it will disappear, levelled by moonquakes or covered with dust thrown out by meteorites hitting the surface.

*"one small step for man;
one giant leap for mankind"*
Neil Armstrong

BRINGING BACK MOON ROCK ►
Armstrong and Aldrin laid out several scientific experiments on the Moon's surface and collected 21.7 kg (48 lb) of lunar rocks and soil. After the astronauts left, the experiments continued working and sending their measurements to Earth by radio. Solar panels supplied electricity to the experiments, which included a seismometer to detect moonquakes.

Overhead hatch for transfer to the command module

Casing for the ascent propulsion fuel tank

◄ THE EAGLE HAS LANDED
Once both astronauts were on the Moon, Aldrin began unloading equipment from Eagle, the lunar module. Eagle's landing, about six hours earlier, nearly didn't happen. As the spacecraft approached its landing site, Armstrong noticed boulders and flew for some distance above the surface looking for a level spot to land on. He finally touched down with only about 20 seconds flying time remaining before the landing would have been called off.

ALDRIN ON THE MOON ►
Aldrin and Armstrong spent more than 21 hours on the Moon, including a moonwalk lasting two and a half hours. Everything was new to them. They kicked the soil to see how deep and dusty it was, tested different ways of moving around in the Moon's weak gravitational field, took photographs, and planted an American flag.

Overboot with ribbed silicone-rubber sole, worn over smaller inner boot

Backpack contains oxygen for Aldrin to breathe and water to keep him cool in his suit

Outer glove fits over an inner glove moulded to Aldrin's hand

Thigh pocket carries tools for experiments and a bag to fill with moondust for analysis

(1) *Eagle's lower half remains on the Moon and acts as a launch pad for the top half, which blasts off to join the CSM.*

(2) *After the astronauts transfer to the CSM, Eagle is cast off. CSM fires its engine to return to Earth.*

(3) *The CSM approaches Earth, and the service module (SM) is jettisoned, leaving the CM with three astronauts inside.*

(4) *Heat shield protects the CM as it descends through Earth's atmosphere.*

(5) *Parachutes open and the CM splashes down in the Pacific Ocean.*

RETURNING TO EARTH ▲

The journey home began with Eagle's ascent stage blasting off from the Moon. The command and service module (CSM), piloted by Michael Collins, had stayed orbiting the Moon. Three hours after Eagle's ascent stage took off, Collins saw the craft approaching, steered towards it, and docked. Eagle was cut adrift and the CSM engine was fired to set a course back to Earth.

▲ SPACE TRAVELLERS IN QUARANTINE

US President Richard Nixon welcomes the crew back to Earth. The astronauts were quarantined (kept apart from other people) inside a sealed, mobile box as soon as they landed in case they had brought any dangerous microbes back with them. They spent the next few weeks in a laboratory where they underwent medical tests and debriefing. Soon after their eventual release, the three heroes were honoured with a huge ticker tape parade in New York City.

SUBSEQUENT MISSIONS

After Apollo 11, six more Apollo missions were launched. All except Apollo 13 landed successfully on different parts of the Moon.

APOLLO 12

Struck by lightning as it took off, but undamaged. Two of the Apollo 12 astronauts landed in the Ocean of Storms in November 1969.

Alan Bean, Apollo 12's lunar module pilot

APOLLO 13

Abandoned its mission to land on the Moon in April 1970 after an explosion in the spacecraft. The crew returned to Earth safely.

APOLLO 14

Landed in Fra Mauro region in February 1971. Apollo 14 was commanded by Alan Shepard, the first US astronaut.

Command module after splashdown

APOLLO 15

Landed in the Hadley-Apennine mountain region of the Moon in July 1971. Apollo 15 was the first of three science missions and the first to take a lunar rover.

APOLLO 16

Landed in the Descartes highlands in April 1972. Apollo 16 was commanded by John Young, the first astronaut to orbit the Moon on two missions (Apollo10 and Apollo 16).

APOLLO 17

Landed between the Taurus mountains and Littrow crater in December 1972. Apollo 17 was the last manned Moon landing.

Astronaut Cernan and lunar rover

SOYUZ PROGRAMME

The Soyuz spacecraft was introduced in 1967. Since then, it has been modified and updated several times. An improved version, called Soyuz TM, was developed in 1986 to transport crews to the Mir space station. Soyuz TMA services the needs of the International Space Station. Most Soyuz spacecraft carry a crew of two or three cosmonauts. An unmanned version, called Progress, is used as a cargo craft to deliver supplies of food, water, and fuel to space stations.

Launch escape system blasts spacecraft clear in an emergency

Fairing protects spacecraft during launch

Soyuz spacecraft carries up to three cosmonauts

LAUNCHING SOYUZ ▶
Moments after lift-off, a Soyuz spacecraft heads for orbit. Soyuz craft are launched by a three-stage rocket. The boosters strapped around the outside form the first stage. The central core is the second stage. The first and second stages are fired together to launch the rocket. Almost five minutes after lift-off, the third stage fires to place the craft in orbit. The rocket can be fitted with a fourth, Fregat, stage to launch satellites and interplanetary probes.

Third stage burns for about 4 minutes

Second/core stage burns for 290 seconds

First stage boosters burn for 118 seconds and then fall away

Descent module contains control systems

Orbital module is the largest module and provides living space

SOYUZ SPACECRAFT ▶
A Soyuz spacecraft is composed of three modules. While the craft is in space, the crew works and sleeps in the orbital module. At one end, this has a mechanism to dock with space stations. At the other end, a hatch gives access to the bell-shaped descent module. The descent module is the only part of a Soyuz craft that returns to Earth. Finally, the instrumentation/propulsion module contains the spacecraft's main engines.

Instrumentation/propulsion module with attached solar arrays

INSIDE SOYUZ ▲
A cosmonaut settles into his seat inside a Soyuz descent module. This module has a habitable volume of 4 m³ (142 cu ft), or about two-thirds the size of an Apollo command module. Each crew member lies on a seat moulded to the shape of his or her body. A good fit is essential to hold the cosmonaut securely for launch and landing. The controls and instruments in the latest Soyuz have been updated to include full-colour computer screens.

Soyuz

Instrumentation module of Soyuz TMA2 spacecraft

Periscope lets crew look forwards and downwards towards Earth

Docking node on a module of the International Space Station

Functional cargo block of International Space Station

Eight thrusters control the descent module during re-entry

Solar array unfolds to 4.2 m (14 ft) long in space

SOYUZ TM SPECIFICATIONS

Orbital module length: 2.6 m (8.5 ft)	
Descent module length: 2.1 m (7 ft)	
Instrument module length: 2.5 m (8 ft)	
Total length: 7 m (23 ft)	
Diameter of habitable modules: 2.2 m (7 ft)	
Maximum diameter: 2.7 m (9 ft)	
Span of solar arrays: 10.6 m (35 ft)	
Habitable volume: 10 m³ (355 cu ft)	
Crew: Two or three	
Mass: 7,070 kg (15,586 lb)	

Orbital module carries rendezvous and docking equipment

Gas tank on outside of an airlock

▲ DOCKING SOYUZ

This Soyuz spacecraft docked with the International Space Station (ISS) in April 2003, after a journey from Earth that took two days. The Expedition Seven crew that it brought to the ISS occupied the space station for the following six months. At that time, Soyuz spacecraft provided the only means of ferrying crews to and from the ISS while NASA's Space Shuttle was grounded after the Columbia accident.

SOYUZ LANDING

PARACHUTES DEPLOYED
After re-entry, a Soyuz descent module releases a series of parachutes to slow its descent in stages. Two pilot parachutes emerge first. The second of these pulls out a drogue chute, which slows the module to less than 300 kph (185 mph). Then the 1,000 m² (11,000 sq ft) main parachute slows it to 25 kph (15 mph).

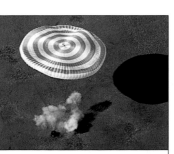

ROCKET BRAKING
The parachute holds the descent module at an angle of 30°, to present the maximum surface area to air-flow and so cool it down. Later, the module is moved into a fully upright position. Just before landing, with the module about 1 m (3 ft) above the ground, six rockets fire to slow its descent to 5 kph (3 mph).

TOUCHDOWN
More than 3 hours after undocking from the rest of the spacecraft, the Soyuz descent module reaches the ground. Shock absorbers built into the crew-members' seats cushion the final bump on landing. Cosmonauts and astronauts have described their landing in the latest type of Soyuz craft as "soft".

RECOVERY
Soyuz descent modules land in the flat steppes of Kazakhstan, northeast of the Baikonur Cosmodrome where Soyuz craft are launched. As soon as a descent module lands, helicopters carrying medical experts arrive. The crew is taken out and helped into reclining chairs before having medical examinations.

SPACE SHUTTLE

The Space Shuttle is the world's first spaceplane. It takes off like a rocket, spends up to a month in orbit, and then lands like an airliner. Travelling at speeds of 28,800 kph (18,000 mph), the Orbiter vehicle can carry a crew of seven astronauts. Its large payload bay carries science experiments and other equipment. A remote arm can be deployed from the bay to launch satellites. Four Orbiters were built, called Columbia, Challenger, Discovery, and Atlantis. Columbia made the first flight on 12 April 1981 from the Kennedy Space Center, Florida. A fifth, Endeavour, was built in 1992.

Shuttle

SHUTTLE SPECIFICATIONS	
Orbiter wingspan: 23.8 m (78 ft)	
Orbiter length: 37.2 m (122 ft)	
Orbiter height: 17.3 m (56 ft)	
Main engines: weigh 3,393 kg (7,480 lb) each	
Maximum speed: 28,800 kph (18,000 mph)	
Weight: 75,000 kg (165,000 lb)	
Payload bay: 18.3 m (160 ft) long by 4.6 m (15 ft) wide	
Crew compartment: 71.5 cubic metres habitable volume	
External Tank: contains 2 million litres (526,000 gallons) of fuel	
Boosters: provide a thrust of 1.5 million kg (3.3 million lb) at take-off	
Total take-off weight: 2 million kg (4.4 million lb)	

SHUTTLE IN ORBIT ▶

In space, the Orbiter opens its payload bay doors. The doors are lined with large panels that work as space radiators. A liquid coolant absorbs heat from equipment inside the Orbiter and then flows through more than 1.5 km (1 mile) of tubing in the radiators. Heat radiates away into space and stops the Orbiter from overheating. Mission specialists can see into the payload bay through windows at the back of the crew compartment.

Launch tower stands 106 m (348 ft) tall, from the ground to the tip of its lightning mast

◀ ON THE LAUNCH PAD
A Space Shuttle on the launch pad is prepared for take-off. It is launched with the help of two Solid Rocket Boosters (SRBs) and a giant External Tank of fuel. When the three main engines in the Orbiter's tail fire, fuel and oxygen pour into them at the rate of 4,000 litres (1,040 gallons) every second. The boosters supply most of the power needed for take-off.

External Tank covered with orange insulating foam

Solid Rocket Boosters provide 71 per cent of the thrust needed to lift the Shuttle

Orbiter is the only part of the Space Shuttle to travel into orbit

Payload bay carries cargo into orbit

FROM EARTH TO SPACE

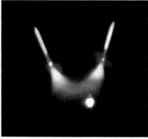

SRB SEPARATION
Two minutes after lift-off, when the Space Shuttle is about 45 km (27 miles) high, its two Solid Rocket Boosters separate and fall away. Rockets in their nose fire to push them away from the Orbiter. They parachute into the Atlantic Ocean 225 km (140 miles) from the shore.

EXTERNAL TANK SEPARATION
Just over eight minutes after lift-off, the Orbiter's main engines shut down and, a few seconds later, the External Tank separates. The tank tumbles back through the atmosphere and breaks up. Any pieces that do not burn up come down in a remote part of the Indian Ocean.

SRBS COLLECTED
When the Shuttle's Solid Rocket Boosters come down in the ocean, they float ready to be collected by ships sent out to retrieve them. The empty rocket casings are returned to their manufacturer and filled with fuel again. They are then sent back to the Kennedy Space Center to be re-used.

ORBITAL INSERTION
The Orbiter is now in an elliptical orbit 65 km (40 miles) to 296 km (184 miles) above Earth. At the highest point, the Orbiter fires its engines to make the orbit circular. Without the External Tank, it cannot use its main engines. Instead it uses two engines in pods either side of its tail.

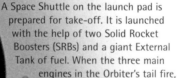

Elevon swivels for steering in Earth's atmosphere

Payload bay can carry satellites, equipment and a laboratory

Orbital engines are used to change orbit

Tail fin with a rudder that doubles as an air brake

Payload bay doors stay open in orbit to cool the Orbiter

INSIDE THE ORBITER ▲

On the flight deck, the mission commander sits in the left seat and the pilot sits in the right seat. The commander is in overall control of the spacecraft and its mission, like an airliner's captain. The pilot assists the commander. The instrument panel in front of them uses similar multi-function display screens to those in the latest airliners. There are two seats for other crew members behind the commander and pilot. Below them, on the mid-deck, there are another three seats.

Wings are short and stubby to withstand re-entry

Flight deck where the commander and pilot fly the Orbiter

Mid-deck work, storage, eating and sleeping area

Radiators inside the doors dump excess heat overboard into space

Thrusters in the nose and tail control the Orbiter's position

Nose cone houses the front landing wheels

▲ CREW EXPLORATION VEHICLE

Scientists and engineers are planning a new orbiter to ferry astronauts and scientists to the Space Station and beyond. Designs include the Crew Exploration Vehicle (CEV) above. This is a capsule similar to that used by the Apollo craft. It is launched by a single-use rocket, rather than a reusable spaceplane. The new CEV will replace the Space Shuttle fleet which is nearing the end of its days. Two Orbiters, Challenger and Columbia, have been lost in accidents, along with their crews.

COUNTDOWN

Preparations for launching a Space Shuttle begin up to three months before lift off and follow a carefully planned sequence of events. The Orbiter is completely overhauled, and its main engines are removed, serviced, and rebuilt, and then rolled out to the launch pad at Kennedy Space Center, Florida. The countdown clock is started 43 hours before take-off. "Holds", when the clock stops for up to four hours, allow time to deal with problems without delaying the launch.

▲ ENGINES FITTED TO ORBITER
The serviced and cleaned main engines are delivered to the Orbiter Processing Facility and refitted in the craft's tail.

▲ EXTERNAL TANK ARRIVES
The huge External Tank arrives by barge from New Orleans. It is hoisted between the boosters on a mobile launch platform.

▲ PAYLOAD INSTALLED
Some of the payload for the mission is installed in the Orbiter's payload bay. This is a robotic arm destined for the ISS.

▲ ORBITER DELIVERED
The Orbiter is ready for its next mission. Its engines, heat-resistant tiles, computers, instruments, and electrical systems have been checked. The Orbiter is now towed to the Vehicle Assembly Building where the engines and fuel tanks are added.

▲ MAKING CONNECTIONS
The Orbiter is bolted to the External Tank at three points. The fuel and electricity supplies are connected between them.

▲ STACK COMPLETED
A crawler transporter moves the completed stack to the launch pad, two or three weeks before launch.

▲ AT THE LAUNCH PAD
With three days to go before launch, the countdown clock is started at T-43 hours (Take-off minus 43 hours).

▲ CREW ENTERS ORBITER
Already in their suits, the crew ride a lift up the launch tower, walk across the crew access arm, and take their seats.

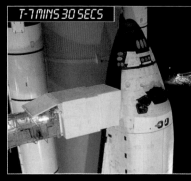

▲ CREW ACCESS ARM RETRACTS
The crew access arm pulls back from the Orbiter. Computers monitor the system thousands of times every second.

▲ SWITCH TO INTERNAL POWER
With 50 seconds left, the Orbiter cuts off electrical power from the outside and switches to its own on-board fuel cells.

▲ MAIN ENGINES FIRE
If the Orbiter's computers detect a problem as the main engines fire, they shut down the engines and halt lift-off.

▲ SOLID BOOSTERS FIRE
Once the two Solid Rocket Boosters fire, it is impossible to switch them off. No one can stop the Shuttle taking off now.

Shuttle

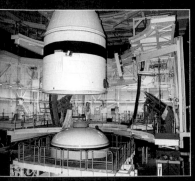

▲ SOLID ROCKET BOOSTERS BUILT
A pair of Solid Rocket Boosters arrive in sections by rail from Utah. They are built in the Vehicle Assembly Building.

28 DAYS

▲ ORBITER HOISTED
A giant crane hoists the 68-tonne Orbiter off the ground and inches it towards the External Tank and boosters.

T-9 MINS

▲ GO/NO-GO FOR LAUNCH
Mission controllers check all data to make a final decision to launch. The clock is re-started at T-9 minutes.

T+2 SECS

▲ LIFT-OFF
As the Solid Rocket Boosters fire, bolts holding the Shuttle down on the launch platform are cut by explosive charges.

▲ "WE HAVE A LIFT-OFF"
Mission time is started at 000:00:00.00 (zero hours, zero minutes, zero seconds). Steam and smoke engulfs the launch pad, as the Shuttle soars away. The mission has begun. As soon as the Shuttle clears the top of the launch tower, about seven seconds after lift-off, control is handed over from the Kennedy Space Center to Mission Control at the Johnson Space Center in Houston, Texas. Here, teams work around the clock on shifts to monitor the Orbiter's systems.

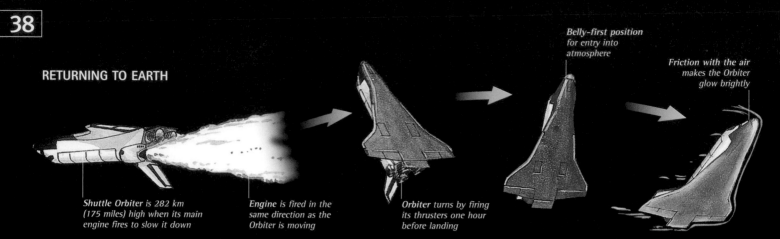

Belly-first position
for entry into
atmosphere

Friction with the air
makes the Orbiter
glow brightly

Shuttle Orbiter is 282 km
(175 miles) high when its main
engine fires to slow it down

Engine is fired in the
same direction as the
Orbiter is moving

Orbiter turns by firing
its thrusters one hour
before landing

COMING HOME

Every spacecraft returning to Earth has to re-enter the atmosphere.
Re-entry begins with an engine burn to slow the craft down, and
gravity then takes over. The Space Shuttle Orbiter dives into the air
at 25,000 kph (15,500 mph), and other craft, past and present, have
had to re-enter at similar speeds. Without protection, spacecraft
would burn up at these speeds. Early manned craft were protected
by heat shields that slowly charred. Soyuz spacecraft still use them
today, but it can be used only once. In contrast, the Shuttle is
protected by a variety of reusable heat-resistant materials.

▲ HEAT-RESISTANT TILES
Almost 25,000 heat-resistant tiles and other
materials cover the Shuttle Orbiter to protect
it from the high temperatures it encounters
during re-entry. The main body of the Orbiter
is made from aluminium, which must be kept
below 175°C (350°F). During re-entry parts of
the spacecraft's surface reach 1,260°C (2,300°F).
The tiles radiate this heat outwards, keeping the
rest of the Orbiter cool.

PROTECTION FROM SCORCHING TEMPERATURES

The Orbiter is covered with materials that can
withstand re-entry many times over. These
materials vary depending on the temperatures
experienced. The nose, the
front edges of the
wings, the front edge
of the tail fin, and the
underside of the Orbiter are
heated the most. The black
ceramic tiles used to cover these
areas provide extra protection.
Thousands of tiles that originally
covered the top and some side areas
of the Orbiter have now been replaced
by lighter sheets of heat-resistant
fabric. The weight saved enables the
Orbiter to carry heavier payloads.

Reinforced carbon-carbon
gives protection against
temperatures of more than
1,260°C (2,300°F).

High-temperature black
insulation tiles protect areas
exposed to temperatures up
to 1,260°C (2,300°F).

Low-temperature white
insulation tiles or insulation
blankets give protection up
to 650°C (1,200°F).

Flexible reusable surface
insulation blankets protect
areas where temperatures
never rise above 370°C (700°F).

Glass, metal alloys with high
melting points, and other
materials are used in other
areas of the Orbiter's surface.

◄ **RIDING THE FLAMES**
As the Orbiter plunges into the atmosphere,
the crew sees flames flashing across the
windows. Thrusters fire to keep the spacecraft at
the right angle. Re-entering belly-first increases drag
and helps to slow the Orbiter down. Sixteen minutes
from touchdown, the Orbiter starts making a series of four
S-shaped turns that slow it down even more. Four minutes
before touchdown, the commander takes over from the
autopilot for the final approach to the runway.

Shuttle

TOUCHDOWN

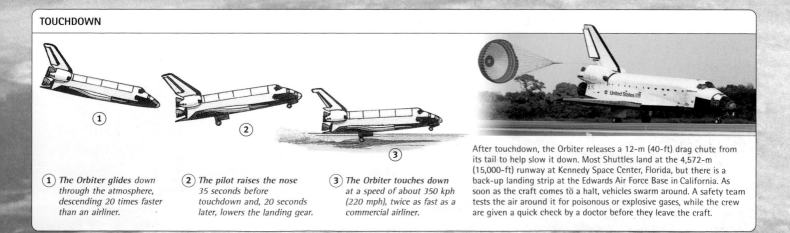

1 *The Orbiter glides* down
through the atmosphere,
descending 20 times faster
than an airliner.

2 *The pilot raises the nose*
35 seconds before
touchdown and, 20 seconds
later, lowers the landing gear.

3 *The Orbiter touches down*
at a speed of about 350 kph
(220 mph), twice as fast as a
commercial airliner.

After touchdown, the Orbiter releases a 12-m (40-ft) drag chute from
its tail to help slow it down. Most Shuttles land at the 4,572-m
(15,000-ft) runway at Kennedy Space Center, Florida, but there is a
back-up landing strip at the Edwards Air Force Base in California. As
soon as the craft comes to a halt, vehicles swarm around. A safety team
tests the air around it for poisonous or explosive gases, while the crew
are given a quick check by a doctor before they leave the craft.

SPACE STATIONS

When the USA won the race to the Moon, the Soviet Union switched its attention to building space stations. Between 1971 and 1982, it launched seven successful Salyut space stations. In 1973, the USA launched its first space station, Skylab. Although damaged during launch, it operated successfully for six years. Then in 1986, the Soviet Union launched the Mir space station. It was constructed in orbit by connecting up a series of modules. During 15 years in space, some of its occupants stayed for more than a year at a time.

Soyuz space ferry carried crews to Salyut 7

Propulsion module contained main engines

Main control console was located here

SALYUT 7 ▲

Salyut 7 was the last Salyut space station. During 50 months in operation, it was visited by 10 different crews and a total of 22 cosmonauts, including French and Indian cosmonauts. In 1986, it was moved to a higher orbit, and some of its equipment was moved to Mir. However, it began to spiral in towards Earth and re-entered the atmosphere earlier than originally expected.

SPECIFICATIONS: SALYUT 7

Length: 14.4 m (47 ft)	
Diameter: 4.15 m (14 ft)	
Mass: 18.9 tonnes	
Launched: 19 April 1982	
Orbit: 279 x 284 km (173 x 176 miles)	
Time in orbit: 8 years 10 months	
Re-entry: 7 February 1991	
Re-entry fate: Burned and broke up over South America, producing an impressive light show; some pieces fell to the ground in Argentina	

Solar arrays for Skylab's solar observatory

Solar observatory studied the Sun

Forward part of workshop contained sleeping compartment

Discoloured exterior of workshop where micrometeoroid shield was torn off

◄ INSIDE SKYLAB

Living conditions inside Skylab were better than in any previous US spacecraft. There was much more room – enough for acrobatics. The crew quarters contained sleep compartments and a ward room where meals were prepared. Skylab's astronauts also had the luxury of a shower, although they rationed its use to once a week, to save water. They used an exercise bike to help counter the effects of weightlessness on their bodies.

◄ SKYLAB

Skylab was made mainly from left-over Apollo hardware. The largest part, the orbital workshop, was the empty third stage of a Saturn V rocket. On launch, one of Skylab's solar panels and a combined micrometeoroid/heat shield were torn off. Astronauts had to make a sunshield to stop the spacecraft overheating. Despite this perilous beginning and the fact that Skylab was only operational for 9 months, its crews took 40,000 pictures of Earth.

SPECIFICATIONS: SKYLAB

Length: 36.12 m (119 ft) when docked with Apollo spacecraft	
Diameter: 6.58 m (22 ft)	
Mass: 76.3 tonnes	
Launched: 14 May 1973	
Orbit: 427 x 439 km (265 x 273 miles)	
Time in orbit: 6 years 2 months	
Re-entry: 11 July 1979	
Re-entry fate: Partially burned up in atmosphere, but some parts came down in the Indian Ocean and western Australia	

Heat radiator for refrigeration system

space
stations

Solar panel of Kvant-1, which was equipped with ultraviolet and X-ray telescopes

Progress supply vessel attached to Kvant-1 module

Solar array attached to Spektr, which had four arrays covering 35 m² (380 sq ft)

Antenna at end of solar array

Core module accommodated up to six cosmonauts

Priroda studied the oceans and atmosphere

Spektr had instruments to study the atmosphere

Docking module for US Space Shuttle to dock with

Soyuz spacecraft ferried crews to and from Mir

Kvant-2 was used for EVAs (extra-vehicular activities or spacewalks)

Soviet manned manoeuvring unit was dumped here at the end of its useful working life

SPECIFICATIONS: MIR

Length: 32.9 m (108 ft) when Soyuz and Progress craft were docked

Diameter: Up to 4.35 m (14 ft) per module

Mass: 135 tonnes

Launched: 20 February 1986 (core module)

Orbit: 385 x 393 km (239 x 244 miles)

Time in orbit: 15 years 1 month

Re-entry: 23 March 2001

Re-entry fate: Partially burned up and broke into several pieces that plunged into the South Pacific Ocean

MIR ▶

Mir was the first space station to be launched in parts and built in space. After the core module was launched in 1986, five more modules and a docking compartment were added over the next 10 years. Kvant-1, added in 1987, was an astronomical observatory. Kvant-2 (1989) was an extension unit with an airlock and scientific instruments. Kristall (1990) was used for materials processing. Spektr (1995) and Priroda (1996) were remote-sensing modules.

INSIDE MIR ▶

The Mir core unit housed the crew's living quarters and a working area. The living quarters contained a hygiene area and a galley, where food was prepared. The hygiene area had a toilet, sink, and shower. The working area contained Mir's control centre. Soyuz spacecraft ferried crews from Earth, and unmanned Progress craft delivered supplies. The US Space Shuttle could also dock with Mir. Several US astronauts stayed in Mir for up to six months.

INTERNATIONAL SPACE STATION

The International Space Station (ISS) is taking shape in Earth orbit and is expected to be finished by around the year 2008. The size of the spacecraft, and the fact that 16 nations are involved in building it, make this the most complex space project ever. The station's main purpose is science. Its internal volume, about the same as that of a Jumbo Jet passenger cabin, will include six laboratories. Crews of up to seven scientists and astronauts will live on the station for up to six months at a time.

Solar panels generate 110 kw of power

▲ CONSTRUCTION TAKES OFF

In November 1998, a Russian Proton rocket carried the Zarya module, the first part of the ISS, into space. In December of the same year, the Space Shuttle Endeavour delivered the Unity module. In July 2000, the Zvezda service module was added. The first crew to live on-board, Expedition One, arrived in November 2000. In February 2001, the Destiny module was delivered by the Space Shuttle Atlantis, and two months later the station's remote manipulator system, a robot arm, arrived.

BUILDING THE SPACE STATION ▲

The ISS is being constructed from pressurized cylindrical sections, called modules, connected together by a framework of beams and towers, called trusses. Parts called nodes have up to six docking ports where several modules can connect together. Spacecraft can dock with vacant ports on the nodes and modules. The USA, Russia, Europe, and Japan are all contributing modules.

Thermal control panels regulate temperature inside the ISS

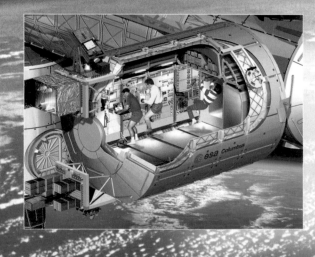

Space tugs deliver supplies of food, water, gases, and fuel

◄ SCIENCE LABORATORY

Astronauts work in shirt-sleeve comfort inside the ISS's laboratories, including the Columbus Laboratory provided by the European Space Agency (ESA). Columbus is a general-purpose science laboratory. Scientists will use it for research in materials, fluids, life sciences, and technology. It can house 10 payload racks, each a complete miniature laboratory. Some experiments will be remotely controlled by scientists working on Earth.

Solar panels rotate to point at the Sun

SPACE DOCKING ▲

Space Shuttles and Soyuz spacecraft have ferried crews to and from the space station up to now, and unmanned Progress spacecraft have delivered supplies. A new space tug is being developed by the European Space Agency. The 20-tonne Automated Transfer Vehicle (ATV) will deliver up to 7.5 tonnes of supplies to the space station every 12 months or so. The unmanned craft will navigate its way to the ISS and dock automatically.

The main truss forms the backbone of the ISS

Pressurized modules provide living quarters and laboratories

ISS SPECIFICATIONS	
Length: 108 m (355 ft)	
Width: 88 m (290 ft)	
Mass: 455 tonnes	
Pressurized volume: 1,200 m³ (42,700 cu ft)	
Solar array wingspan: 73 m (240 ft)	
Solar array area: 4,000 m² (43,000 sq ft)	
Orbital speed : 28,000 kph (17,400 mph)	
Orbit: 400 km (249 miles) above Earth's surface	
Orbital period: About 92 minutes	
First resident crew: 2 November 2000	
Size of crew: Between 3 and 7	

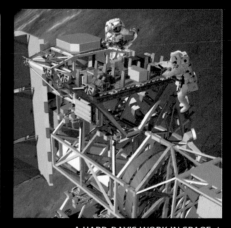

A HARD DAY'S WORK IN SPACE ▲

Two astronauts cling onto a section of the station's skeletal frame as they complete another hard day's work on the biggest building site in space. The ISS is being constructed from more than 100 different parts launched by 45 space missions. About 160 spacewalks lasting nearly 1,000 hours will be needed to connect all the parts together. Once the station is finished, astronauts will continue to make spacewalks to service external experiments and to perform routine maintenance.

Spacecraft dock at ports in several positions

Radiators turn edge-on to the Sun to lose excess heat

Remote sensing instruments look down on Earth

Solar arrays are the biggest and most powerful ever used in space

ISS

THE BODY IN SPACE

Humans have evolved to work best in the atmosphere and gravity that exist on the Earth's surface. To survive in space, astronauts have to take an Earth-like environment with them. Fresh oxygen is circulated around the craft for them to breathe. The main difference in space is the weightlessness causing astronauts to float around. As soon as astronauts go into space, their bodies start adapting to this weightlessness. Muscles, bones, heart, and blood all undergo changes. At the end of a lengthy spaceflight, astronauts have to adapt to living with weight again.

e ▶▶
life in space

FEELING WEIGHTLESS ▶
Floating about inside a spacecraft looks fun, but at least half of all astronauts suffer an unpleasant reaction to weightlessness. On Earth, gravity exerts a force on our bodies, which gives us weight and keeps us rooted to the ground. It also pulls body fluid downwards. In space, astronauts lose their sense of balance. They can also feel sick, and go off food. It can take two weeks for the digestive system to fully adjust. NASA plans no spacewalks during the first three days of a mission, because an astronaut who vomits inside a spacesuit risks suffocation.

INSIDE AN ASTRONAUT'S BODY

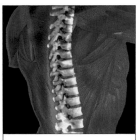

STRETCHING SPINES
Astronauts are taller in space than they are on Earth. Gravity normally pulls the vertebrae, the bones of the spine, close together. In space, vertebrae can spread out a little more, lengthening the spine. This effect makes the astronaut 30–60 mm (around 2 in) taller, and slimmer-looking. It is not a lasting effect. An astronaut's height returns to normal when he or she comes back to Earth.

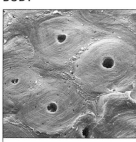

WEAKENED BONE
Bones become weaker because they no longer need to support the body weight. This bone cross section shows minerals densely packed in rings to give them strength. Blood vessels run through the centre. In space, calcium dissolves out of the bones into the blood. This makes bones more brittle. Astronauts returning to Earth after a long mission are more likely to suffer a bone fracture.

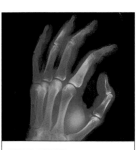

SPACE AGEING
In the 1980s, scientists realized that weightlessness affects the body in a similar way to ageing. Bones lose their mass in space over long periods, just as ageing bones become thinner. Loss of bone calcium is similar to a condition called osteoporosis that affects some older people, usually women. By studying the effects of weightlessness, scientists can understand the ageing process.

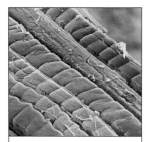

WASTING MUSCLES
Without the full force of gravity to work against, an astronaut's muscles quickly begin to atrophy (waste). They become smaller and weaker. The large weight-bearing muscles in the legs are affected the most, because they are used the least in space. Fortunately, most of the muscle lost during a spaceflight is rebuilt within a month of returning to Earth.

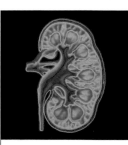

INTERNAL ORGANS
Some of the body's internal organs change or feel different in weightlessness. Astronauts often say their stomach feels fuller, possibly because their digestive system is breaking down food more slowly. The kidneys have to work harder. They remove waste materials from the blood, including calcium lost from the bones. Extra calcium can form painful lumps called kidney stones.

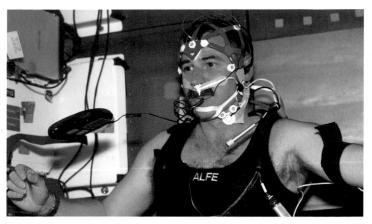

▲ MONITORING HEALTH

Many astronauts report problems sleeping for long periods in space, perhaps because of the excitement and pressures of the the mission, or the constant noise inside the craft. This Shuttle astronaut is taking part in a sleep experiment. He is fitted with a set of sensors to monitor his brainwave activity, and a sensor suit to study his breathing as he sleeps. Sensors stuck to the skin pick up the body's electrical activity, which is transmitted to Earth and monitored by doctors at mission control.

BIOLOGICAL EFFECTS OF LACK OF GRAVITY

Bones: Astronauts lose up to 6% of bone mass while in space, at the rate of 1-2% a month

Blood: Up to 17% of blood volume is lost after just 2-3 days

Muscles: Up to 20% of muscle mass is lost, at the rate of 5% a week

Teeth: Less saliva is produced in space, causing plaque build-up – astronauts chew gum to help them produce saliva

Nose and eyes: Astronauts sneeze a lot – as much as 30 times an hour – and suffer eye irritations. This is because of the dust and shed human skin cells floating around the craft

Head: About a litre of extra fluid moves up to the head, so astronauts feel as though they have a head cold

ESSENTIAL EXERCISE ▶

This astronaut uses a cycling machine, part of the daily exercise routine lasting two hours or more. Astronauts exercise to minimize the effects of weightlessness on their body. Their figures change in space because of muscle wastage and fluids moving upwards. Legs are particularly affected – they get thinner, a condition known as bird legs. Normal treadmills, rowing machines, and exercise bikes are useless in space, because astronauts would just float off them. Space exercise machines have straps or elastic ropes to hold the astronaut down and give their muscles something to work against.

Hand-held weights exercise hand and arm muscles

Cycling prevents bones and muscles wasting

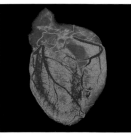

SHRINKING HEART

The heart is a muscle, so in space it wastes just like the leg muscles. It normally pumps blood against gravity. In space, it has less work to do. As a result, it shrinks in size. It also slows down and pumps less blood each time it beats. Although astronauts feel normal in space, these changes reduce their ability to do hard physical work for long periods when they return to Earth.

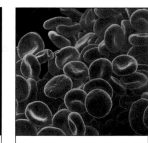

LOSING BLOOD CELLS

Gravity normally pulls blood down towards the feet. In space, it spreads out evenly throughout the body. There is more blood than usual from the waist up. The body tries to reduce the amount of blood in the head by slowing down the heart. Astronauts also lose about 20% of red blood cells which causes anaemia and tiredness. This can last for two or more years after the trip.

24 HOURS IN SPACE

Each day of a space mission is planned in meticulous detail. Space Shuttle trips are planned to the last second, long before the crew leaves Earth. Crews on longer missions to the International Space Station have a basic plan, which is modified during daily conferences between the crew and ground controllers. Plans have to be adaptable to allow for problems with equipment or jobs taking longer in space. Essential exercise is written into the daily mission plan, along with a little time for play.

▲ 05:30 – WAKEY, WAKEY!
International Space Station astronauts are woken up by an alarm buzzer, but music plays to wake up Shuttle crews.

▲ 06:10 – IN THE GALLEY
The first meal of the day might be fruit and cereal followed by coffee or tea and a roll – all eaten straight from the pack.

▲ 07:00 – WORK PREPARATION
Each morning a detailed, timed plan of the day's work is drawn up in conjunction with ground controllers.

▲ 07:45 – ALL SYSTEMS GO
First work sessions include monitoring vital spacecraft systems and performing routine maintenance jobs.

▲ 07:55 – EXERCISE
Daily exercise sessions, lasting up to an hour, work muscles that otherwise do not get used in micro-gravity.

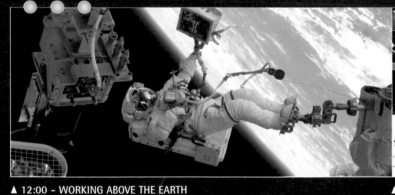

▲ 12:00 – WORKING ABOVE THE EARTH
Extra Vehicular Activity (EVA) involves going outside the spacecraft to carry out repairs or to assemble parts of the ISS. Some EVAs last two to three hours. Many spacewalkers can spend their entire working day outside on a tiring seven-hour shift.

▲ 13:35 – A WORKING LUNCH
The crew gather in the galley for lunch, although busy Shuttle schedules mean astronauts often snack while working.

▲ 14:50 – INTERVIEWS
TV and radio shows, or webcasts, are part of the job. Astronauts give interviews from space to journalists on Earth.

▲ 18:10 – BACK TO WORK
The spacecraft serves as a workshop and a science laboratory. Each crew takes its own set of tools for their mission.

▲ 18:15 – CONFERENCE
The crew get together to discuss how the day's work has progressed and make any necessary changes to the schedule.

▲ 19:00 – DINNER IS SERVED
Two astronauts eat rice with chopsticks on mid-deck. They choose their meals months in advance, before leaving Earth.

▲ 20:00 – LEISURE
It's finally time to relax. Astronauts take their own books and CDs, watch DVDs, and sometimes play instruments.

▲ 05:40 – WASH AND GO
Water is limited in space, so astronauts stay clean by using washcloths and rinseless soap and shampoo.

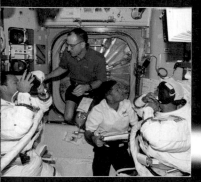

▲ 09:25 – PREPARING FOR AN EVA
Two astronauts don their spacesuits in preparation for a spacewalk, helped and closely monitored by crew members.

▲ 17:10 – MORE EXERCISE
Back to the exercise bike or treadmill for the second work-out, to tone up the muscles and protect against weak bones.

▲ 21:00 – SLEEP
After a demanding day's work, the astronauts strap themselves into sleeping bags for an eight hour sleep.

● HERE COMES THE SUN ... AGAIN!
Our lives on Earth are regulated by the 24-hour day and night cycle. Sunrises mark the start of each day and darkness signals night's arrival. In space, astronauts see the Sun rise and set far more often. The number of sunrises depends on the spacecraft's speed and that depends on its height. A spacecraft 500 km (310 miles) above the Earth is travelling at 28,800 kph (18,000 mph). This means it orbits roughly once every 90 minutes, so astronauts see 16 sunrises every 24 hours.

e ▸▸
life in space

THE NIGHT SHIFT ▶
Astronauts work on the Hubble Space Telescope, bathed in the rosy glow of the Shuttle's lights as the last rays of sunshine retreat behind the Earth. With a sunrise every 90 minutes, astronauts spend many periods in darkness with just the lights of the craft to illuminate their work. But they also see several sunrises during a long spacewalk. Astronauts describe a sunrise in space as a rainbow of light bursting from the horizon like an erupting volcano.

LIVING IN SPACE

Living in space is a bit like living with several other people in a cramped caravan. Astronauts work hard, but they don't have to do some of the daily chores that have to be done on Earth. One-use food containers means there is no washing up to do. Clothes don't have to be cleaned either, because astronauts wear disposable clothes. Rubbish is disposed of in an unusual way. Space Station astronauts load their rubbish into empty supply ships. These unmanned craft are then steered into the atmosphere and burn up.

LONGLIFE TINNED FOOD

DRIED FOOD WITH TUBE FOR WATER

▲ EATING IN SPACE
Astronauts on early missions ate unappetizing meals of paste-like food squeezed from tubes, or dried meat cubes coated with gelatine to trap crumbs. Choices on the space menu today range from breakfast cereals and fresh fruit to beefsteak. Astronauts have a poor sense of taste in space, so they prefer highly flavoured and spiced foods. Ketchup or spicy sauce are often added to meals, which are heated in an on-board oven.

VACUUM-PACKED FRESH FOOD

◄ PACKAGING FOOD FOR SPACE
Space food is packaged in air-tight containers to keep it fresh until needed. Foods sterilized by heat are supplied in metal tins or pouches. Irradiated and low-moisture foods, such as dried apricots, are sealed in foil. Foods that have to be re-hydrated have plastic containers with tubes to inject water. Fresh foods, such as nuts and biscuits, are packed in plastic pouches. Drinks come in squeeze bottles, or as powders to be mixed with water.

SPACE MENU	
Breakfast	Cereal with raisins (re-hydratable with water)
	Breakfast roll (fresh food)
	Pears (thermostabilized – heat-treated to preserve)
	Vanilla breakfast drink (beverage)
	Tea or coffee (beverage)
Lunch	Chicken strips in salsa (thermostabilized)
	Macaroni and cheese (re-hydratable)
	Rice with butter (thermostabilized)
	Macadamia nuts (fresh)
	Apple cider (beverage)
Dinner	Shrimp cocktail (re-hydratable)
	Beef steak (irradiated, treated with radiation to preserve)
	Macaroni & cheese (re-hydratable)
	Fruit cocktail (thermostabilized)
	Strawberry drink (beverage)

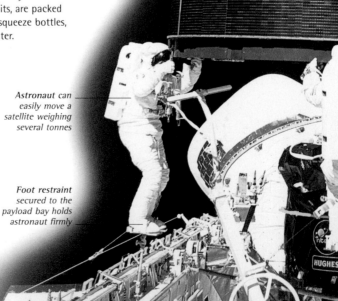

Satellite's antenna used to send and receive data

Antenna dish opens once the satellite is in place

Astronaut can easily move a satellite weighing several tonnes

Foot restraint secured to the payload bay holds astronaut firmly

▲ KEEPING CLEAN

Early astronauts didn't wash at all. Space missions last much longer today, so hygiene is important. The Skylab space station had a shower, but showers are not effective in space. As water doesn't fall in orbit, a fan has to blow the water at the bather, and users have to be careful not to let droplets escape to float around. Usually, astronauts use wet cloths and rinseless cleansing liquids to keep clean and brush their teeth as they would on Earth.

▲ LIVING IN MICROGRAVITY

Working astronauts have to anchor themselves behind rails so they don't float away from their workstation. Weightlessness makes it easy to move around, but it also presents problems. Nothing stays where an astronaut puts it. The tiniest movement can send something floating across the spacecraft. Everything has to be held down by hook-and-loop pads or straps, or be put away. There is no defined floor or ceiling in the Shuttle – equipment is arranged over all surfaces, so crew have to orientate themselves.

GROWING PLANTS IN SPACE ▶

Future space missions may depend on plants to provide food and recycle water and air. Normally, gravity makes plant roots grow downwards and shoots grow upwards. Without gravity, plants can't sense which way to grow, so the plants and their roots grow in all directions. They have to be watered in a different way too, because weightless water doesn't sink into soil or plant. It rests on the plant or soil in bubbles.

life in space

Remote Manipulator System arm provides a mobile platform

◀ WORKING IN SPACE

Launching and servicing satellites is part of an astronaut's job. While working outside, the crew are always clipped to a foot restraint or safety line to stop them floating away. Once secure, they can do things in space that are impossible on Earth. Weightlessness means that an astronaut can move an enormous object by hand, such as this 800-kg (1,760-lb) satellite. However, when a massive object starts moving, a lot of force is needed to stop it.

▲ SLEEPING ARRANGEMENTS

The Shuttle crew work in shifts, so some sleep while others work during their day. Eye and ear plugs are essential. They stick their sleeping bags to a wall to stop them floating off and banging into things. Despite the lack of a bed, astronauts report that they still turn over in their sleep. The Shuttle commander often sleeps on the flight deck in case a problem arises. On the ISS, the crew sleeps at the same time and there are two 'bedroom' areas.

SPACEWALKS

Astronauts routinely go on spacewalks, or EVAs (Extra-Vehicular
Activities), to work outside. Leaving the safety of the spacecraft to
walk outside, 400 km (245 miles) or so above Earth, is dangerous.
It takes 15 minutes to put on a spacesuit, but it takes much longer
to prepare to leave the craft. A spacesuit supplies pure oxygen at
less than one third the air pressure inside the spacecraft. A sudden
drop in pressure, from the cabin to the spacesuit, could cause a
condition called decompression sickness that can be fatal. The
pressure inside the craft has to be lowered gradually, over
several hours, before it is safe for an astronaut to go outside.

*Remote manipulator
arm (robot arm) has
six joints and is
15 m (50ft) long*

*Portable life support
system supplies oxygen
for up to seven hours*

*Helmet light bar
mounted on the
helmet to give
extra illumination*

*Face visor is sprayed
with an anti-fog
solution inside, so it
doesn't mist up*

*Tool clips hold
tools while they
are not in use*

*Pistol grip tool is
computer controlled to
set precise speed, force,
and number of turns*

▲ THE FIRST SPACEWALK
On 18 March 1965, Alexei Leonov became the first person to
walk in space. During Voskhod 2's second orbit, Leonov crawled
through an inflatable airlock and floated out into space 500 km
(310 miles) above Earth, at the end of a 5-metre (16-foot) safety
line. Ten minutes later he tried to go back inside, but couldn't
squeeze into the airlock as his suit had ballooned in the vacuum.
He eventually let air out of his suit and squeezed in head first.

PERFORMING AN EVA ▶
A Shuttle spacesuit's life support system
supplies enough oxygen to last seven hours,
but spacewalks can be even longer. In 2001,
two astronauts made a spacewalk lasting almost
nine hours by plugging into the Space Shuttle's main life
support system for two hours. Astronauts performing
EVAs are constantly monitored by cameras, other
astronauts, and ground controllers. It can be tricky to
tell which astronaut is which, so their spacesuits have
coloured stripes on the legs to help identify them.

◀ ED WHITE
Less than three months after Leonov's
historic spacewalk, Ed White became
the first US spacewalker. On 3 June
1965, he opened his Gemini 4 hatch
and pulled himself out. He spent about
20 minutes outside, filmed by fellow
crewman James McDivitt. White
experimented with moving himself
around by using jets of gas from a
handheld gas-gun. When he got back inside,
he had trouble with the hatch. McDivitt had to hold
onto White's legs while he closed and locked it!

▲ FLYING FREE

During EVAs, astronauts are tethered so they don't float away, but they can fly free using gas-jet-propelled backpacks. The Manned Manoeuvring Unit (MMU) was used on early Shuttle flights. A smaller SAFER unit (Simplified Aid For Extravehicular activity Rescue) has been developed for the ISS. Astronauts who drift away from the station can propel themselves back by using a joystick control to expel jets of nitrogen gas from the unit's 24 nozzles.

Checklist pad fitted onto the sleeve holds up to 27 pages of information

Coloured stripes on spacesuits identify individual astronauts

Foot restraint prevents the astronaut from floating away

space walks

Gripping teeth stop parts turning the wrong way

▲ STANDING THEIR GROUND

Weightlessness makes it easy to move around, but it also presents a problem for astronauts trying to work. If they push something, they just fly back in the opposite direction. They have to anchor themselves in place using a foot restraint, leaving both hands free for work. The ISS has sockets all over it where foot restraints can be plugged in. Astronauts can also anchor themselves to the Space Shuttle's remote manipulator arm which serves as a manoeuvrable but stable platform to work on.

SPACE TOOLS ►

Tools used by spacewalking astronauts may look similar to standard ones, but they are designed for the job. Bulky space gloves are pressurized with air. This makes it harder for astronauts to grip, so tools have bigger handles. Even tightening a nut can be tricky, as the astronaut and not the nut may turn, and the loosened nut floats off. Cordless power tools used on Earth were invented for space, as they need little exertion to use, and no electric cables.

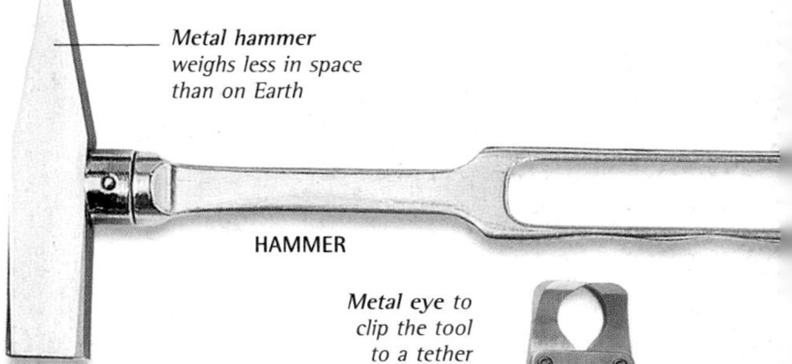

Metal hammer weighs less in space than on Earth

HAMMER

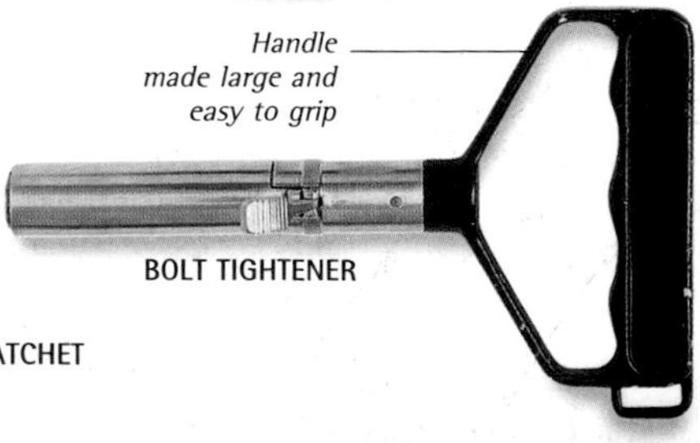

Metal eye to clip the tool to a tether

Handle made large and easy to grip

BOLT TIGHTENER

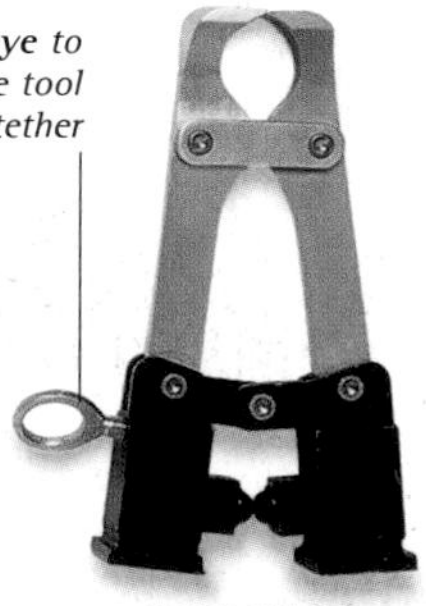

RATCHET

WIRE CUTTER

SPACESUITS

A spacesuit is more than a set of work clothes, it's a survival system. If astronauts stepped out into space without any protection, they would be unconscious within 15 seconds and all their body fluids would bubble and freeze. A spacesuit not only supplies oxygen to breathe, it also protects the astronaut from the vacuum of space, from temperature extremes of 121°C (250°F) to -156°C (-250°F), and from meteorite particles. There are two types of spacesuit. One is worn during take-off and re-entry, the other for spacewalks.

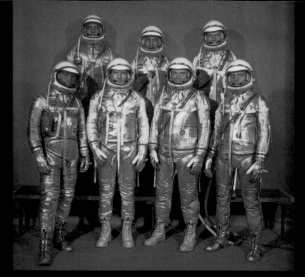

▲ THE MERCURY SPACESUIT
Spacesuits worn by Mercury astronauts in the early 1960s were developed from pressure suits designed for Navy pilots in the 1950s. The suit, worn over long-john underwear, was made from three layers of nylon. The outer layer was impregnated with aluminium to give better flame resistance. It was worn with gloves, helmet, lace-up flying boots, and oxygen was supplied for the astronaut to breathe. The suit was not pressurized unless the Mercury capsule lost cabin pressure.

Boots are made as part of the suit to stop air leaking out

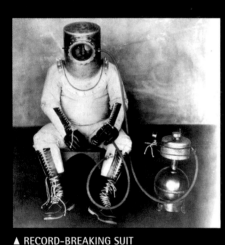

▲ RECORD-BREAKING SUIT
The first pressurized suit worn by a pilot was made for the record-breaking American aviator, Wiley Post, in 1934. He found he could go faster by flying higher, so had a pressure suit made to let him fly in thin air for longer. It was made of rubber covered by cotton, with a metal helmet and an oxygen supply. The suit was produced by B. F. Goodrich, the company that later made the Mercury astronauts' spacesuits.

DRESSING FOR A SPACEWALK

LEGS FIRST
A Space Shuttle astronaut wearing a Liquid Cooling and Ventilation Garment steps into the spacesuit's Lower Torso Assembly (LTA).

SLIDING INTO THE TOP
Next, the astronaut rises into the suit's Hard Upper Torso (HUT), which normally hangs on the wall of the Space Shuttle's airlock.

LOCKING UP
The two halves of the suit are locked together. Helmet and gloves are added and locked in place. Then the pressure inside the suit is adjusted.

▲ SHUTTLE EVA SUIT
The spacesuit worn by Shuttle astronauts on spacewalks is called the EMU (Extravehicular Mobility Unit). Most of the suit is made from 11 layers of different coated, non-coated, and aluminized materials, many of them invented for use in space. It houses a water cooling system, drink bag, and urine collection device. On Earth, the suit weighs up to 47 kg (104 lb) and the life support system another 67 kg (148 lb). With the camera, it weighs a total of 117.6 kg (260 lb).

(1) *Tough outer layer is a mixture of three fire-retardant fibres, Gore-Tex, Kevlar, and Nomex, to protect against heat and puncture.*

(2) *The five-layer Thermal Micrometeoroid Garment Liner (TMG), made from aluminium-coated fabric, deflects the Sun's heat.*

(3) *The TMG is lined with a layer of material made from neoprene-coated (rubberized) nylon to prevent damage from micrometeoroids.*

(4) *The restraint layer, made from Dacron, stops the pressure bladder inside it from blowing up like a balloon. Its pattern aids bending.*

(5) *The innermost layer of the spacesuit is known as the bladder. It is pressurized and airtight, as seams are heat-sealed and overtaped.*

(6) *The Liquid Cooling and Ventilation Garment is a two-layer suit made from nylon. It stretches by 300% to fit snugly to the body.*

(7) *Cool water flows through 91.44 m (300 ft) of plastic tubing laced between the layers of the Cooling and Ventilation Garment.*

space suits

Thick gloves have rubber fingertips to help astronauts grip

Loops and clips for attaching tools to stop them floating away

Outer shell is shiny, white Gore-Tex fabric to minimize heat absorbtion

Display and control Module monitors the life support system

Helmet visor is gold-coated to cut glare from sunlight

Helmet is made of a hard, durable polycarbonate material

Space tools are two to three times larger to be held in bulky gloves

Cameras and lights are fitted on each side of the helmet

Radio aerial sends and receives radio communications signals

Life support system contains oxygen tanks, cooling water, and radios

Spacesuit becomes rigid when pressurized (inflated) so flexible areas are included at the joints

Headset contains microphones and earphones

◄ LAUNCH SUIT

A distinctive orange spacesuit is worn by Shuttle astronauts during launch and re-entry. It protects astronauts from loss of cabin pressure and the very low air or water temperatures they could encounter if they bailed out of the Orbiter. During landing, the suit squeezes the astronaut's middle and legs to stop blood pooling in the legs after a long period in space. It also has a satellite beacon and flares, to help locate crew in water.

◄ THE SOYUZ SPACESUIT

Soyuz cosmonauts wear the Sokol (Falcon) spacesuit for take-off and landing. The pressure suit is covered with white nylon canvas, with a hood and hinged visor. Air and coolant hoses, and electric cables can connect to the suit's body. Two chest labels show the cosmonaut's name in the Russian Cyrillic alphabet and the Roman alphabet. The spacesuit worn by cosmonauts for spacewalks is called the Orlan (Eagle) suit.

Metal rings on the sleeves lock onto detachable gloves

TRAINING FOR SPACE

When a space agency invites applications from people who want to be astronauts, thousands of people reply. Only one in 200 is accepted. After an initial year's basic training, the successful candidates become astronauts, but they may have to wait several years before going into space. During that time, they continue taking training courses. When they are allocated a mission, they begin intensive training for that specific mission, often using simulators – mock-ups of the craft or equipment they will have to use in space. Crews often say a real mission is easy compared to their training sessions in simulators.

e ▶▶ training

Astronaut floats as if weightless

◄ FLIGHT TRAINING
Pilot astronauts keep their flying skills up to scratch by flying NASA's T-38 jets regularly during training. The T-38 is a two-seat training jet. Mission and payload specialists fly in the back seat to get experience of using navigation and communications systems. The Shuttle lands without engine power, so the pilot has only one chance to land it. Pilot astronauts practise landing in simulators and in the Shuttle Training Aircraft, a converted Gulfstream business jet.

Eyepieces display a computer-generated view of inside a craft

Gloves sense hand positions

VOMIT COMET ▶
An astronaut can experience weightlessness without having to go into space, by using an aircraft known as the Vomit Comet! The KC-135 climbs steeply upwards and then dives, over and over again. As it tips over the top of each climb, the plane and everything inside is in free-fall (moving around without restraint), so everyone inside becomes weightless for up to 25 seconds. It can also simulate lunar and Martian gravity.

◄ VIRTUAL SPACE
This astronaut is using a Virtual Reality (VR) training system. VR is used to train astronauts without having to use a simulator. The astronaut sees a computer-generated version of equipment displayed on screens in front of his eyes. He might see part of the ISS or the Shuttle payload bay. He can move about in the virtual space and he can pick up virtual objects and move them around, because his gloves have sensors linked to the screens.

◄ UNDERWATER TRAINING

NASA's Neutral Buoyancy Laboratory is one of the world's largest swimming pools. It's 31 m (202 ft) long, 31 m (102 ft) wide, and 12.5 m (40 ft) deep, and contains 20 million litres (6 million gallons) of water. It's big enough to hold a full-size mock-up of the Shuttle payload bay. Astronauts use the tank to train for EVAs (spacewalks). The buoyancy of the water lets them float as if they were in space.

Full-size equipment is used in the training tank

Air bags make equipment float as if weightless

Video cameras record progress in the tank

Divers prepare equipment and act as lifeguards

ASTRONAUT SELECTION AND TRAINING DATA

Career backgrounds: Three types of astronauts take part in space missions – pilots, mission specialists, and payload specialists

Pilot astronauts: The commander and pilot – the astronauts who fly the spacecraft. They must have clocked up at least 1,000 hours' experience of flying jet aircraft

Mission specialists: Coordinate all on-board operations, perform spacewalks, and handle the payload

Payload specialists: Chosen from scientists or engineers outside NASA to carry out particular experiments or operate specific payloads

Numbers: NASA takes 20-30 new candidates every two years

Selection: The process takes about eight months and includes interviews, medical examinations and orientation tests

Training: There is a minimum of 2 years' training before they are assigned a flight. They then train for up to a year for that mission

Height: Candidates are usually between 160 cm and 185 cm (64 and 76 in) tall

Education: Most astronauts have an advanced (Master's) degree

▲ SCIENTIST ASTRONAUTS

Until 1972, all astronauts were pilots. They were trained to carry out specific scientific experiments for their missions. In 1972, the Apollo 17 lunar module pilot was Dr Harrison Schmitt, (above), a trained geologist. Schmitt conducted tests to find out if the Moon was volcanically active. Since then, astronauts have come from a variety of backgrounds, among them many highly trained scientists who are assigned missions because of the experiments that will be taking place on board.

FLIGHT SIMULATORS ▼

Soyuz crews train for missions in the Soyuz cockpit simulator in Star City – the Russian space training centre, near Moscow. Pilot astronauts practise their missions hundreds of times in simulators, which have identical controls and displays to those in the spacecraft. US Space Shuttle crews train in the Shuttle Mission Simulator in Houston, where they can practise launch, ascent, and docking. A straight up 90° tilt simulates acceleration and take-off.

◄ SURVIVAL TRAINING

Emergency training includes a parachute course and how to use the survival suit used in the spacecraft. Astronauts who bail out would probably land in water or in a remote place on land, so they also take survival courses, in case they are marooned for days. Soyuz spacecraft are used as emergency escape vehicles on the International Space Station, so US astronauts visit Russia to train in Soyuz simulators too.

SPACE RESCUE

Spacecraft designers and mission planners work hard to make space missions as safe as possible. However, rockets are so powerful, fuel is so explosive, and spacecraft are such complex machines that accidents still happen. Apollo 13 was launched at 13:13 Houston time on 11 April 1970. On 13 April, 330,000 km (205,000 miles) from Earth, the crew heard a bang. An oxygen tank had exploded. The spacecraft quickly lost power and oxygen. Engineers, scientists, and astronauts fought for four days to bring the spacecraft home.

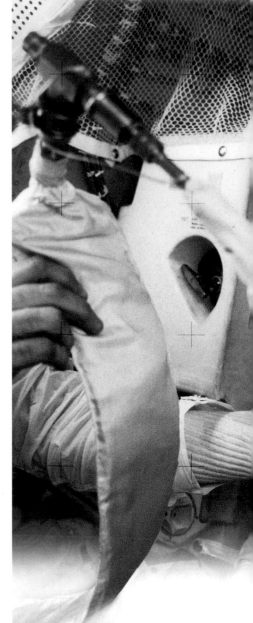

A SOLUTION FROM HOUSTON ▶
Mission control instructed the Apollo 13 crew to power down the command module, to save it for re-entry, and move into the lunar module (LM). With three astronauts instead of the two it was designed for, the LM's chemical air scrubber could not cope. Spare filter cartridges from the command module would not fit the LM's air filters. Engineers on Earth had to design something to take carbon dioxide out of the air using only items the astronauts had with them.

"Houston, we've had a problem"

Jack Swigert, command module pilot

A MAKESHIFT REPAIR ▶
Conditions in the lunar module were cramped, cold, and uncomfortable. It was equipped to support two men for less than 50 hours. The three Apollo 13 astronauts would be inside for at least 84 hours. The amount of carbon dioxide in the air, from the crew breathing out, started rising. Following step-by-step instructions from ground control, John Swigert (far right) and James Lovell had to make an air filter using spare cartridges, a plastic bag, an air hose from a spacesuit, and sticky tape. It worked.

THE ROUTE HOME

Mission controllers debated whether to turn Apollo 13 round and bring it straight home or let it continue around the Moon. They decided that firing the service module's engine to come home was risky. Sending the spacecraft around the Moon was also risky as it had only half the electrical power it needed for the return journey. The craft continued to the Moon, using the lunar module's engine to put the craft back on course for Earth. This shows Apollo 13's route from take-off at 000:00:00.

Apollo 13's flight path

1 *004:01:00 (hours, mins, secs)*
Command and service module docks with the lunar module on the way to the Moon.

4 *077:33:10*
The spacecraft reappears from behind the Moon, 25 minutes after disappearing behind it.

2 *030:40:49*
A mid-course correction puts Apollo 13 on course for its Moon landing.

5 *105:18:28*
The lunar module engine is fired for 14 seconds to fine-tune the spacecraft's course.

7 *140:10:00*
The command module is powered up for re-entry into the Earth's atmosphere.

3 *055:54:53*
The crew hears a loud bang as an oxygen tank explodes. Two hours later, they enter the lunar module.

6 *138:01:48*
The wrecked service module is jettisoned. The crew see, and photograph, the damage for the first time.

8 *141:30:00*
The lunar module is discarded and the command module begins its journey through the atmosphere.

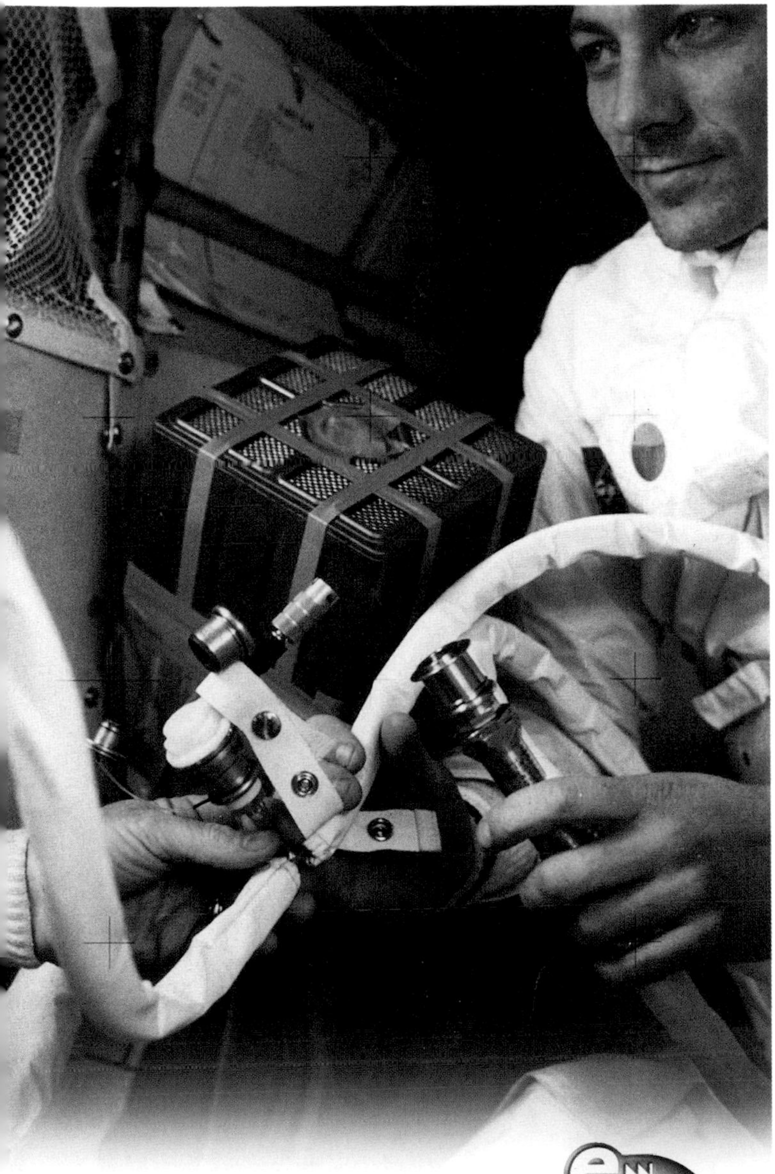

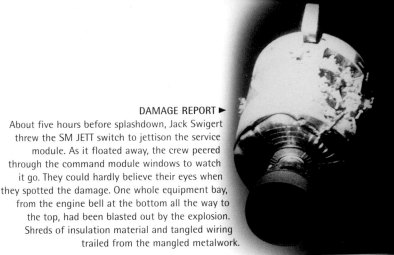

DAMAGE REPORT ▶

About five hours before splashdown, Jack Swigert threw the SM JETT switch to jettison the service module. As it floated away, the crew peered through the command module windows to watch it go. They could hardly believe their eyes when they spotted the damage. One whole equipment bay, from the engine bell at the bottom all the way to the top, had been blasted out by the explosion. Shreds of insulation material and tangled wiring trailed from the mangled metalwork.

▲ SPLASHDOWN

As the command module re-entered Earth's atmosphere, the usual four-minute radio black-out began. Controllers hoped the command module was undamaged or the crew would not survive. After four minutes, they called the crew. After 33 tense seconds, they answered. Minutes later, the command module landed. The crew was flown to safety and the command module was hoisted out of the sea.

e ▸▸
space
rescue

*"Gentlemen,
it's been a privilege
flying with you"*

James Lovell

RETURN TO EARTH ▶

Lovell, Swigert, and Fred Haise were cheered by sailors as they stepped from the recovery helicopter onto the *USS Iwo Jima*'s deck. Below decks they were given medical examinations. Haise was suffering from a kidney infection and a high fever caused by the freezing conditions and shortage of water in the spacecraft. All three astronauts were dehydrated, tired, and they had lost weight. Lovell lost more than 6 kg (13.2 lb) in six days.

INVESTIGATION TECHNIQUES

If a spacecraft fails in space, investigators may never know the cause. If it fails in the atmosphere, the wreckage is studied closely for clues.

The Space Shuttle Orbiter Columbia broke up while re-entering the atmosphere on 1 February, 2003. Wreckage fell over 72,000 km² (27,800 sq miles) of the USA. Every piece found was collected and brought to the Kennedy Space Center, where it was laid out on a hangar floor. Investigators also studied data received from the Orbiter, a film of the launch, and images from space. They concluded that insulation falling from the external tank had damaged Columbia's left wing, causing the Orbiter to break up during re-entry. Discovering the cause means that a similar accident can be prevented in future.

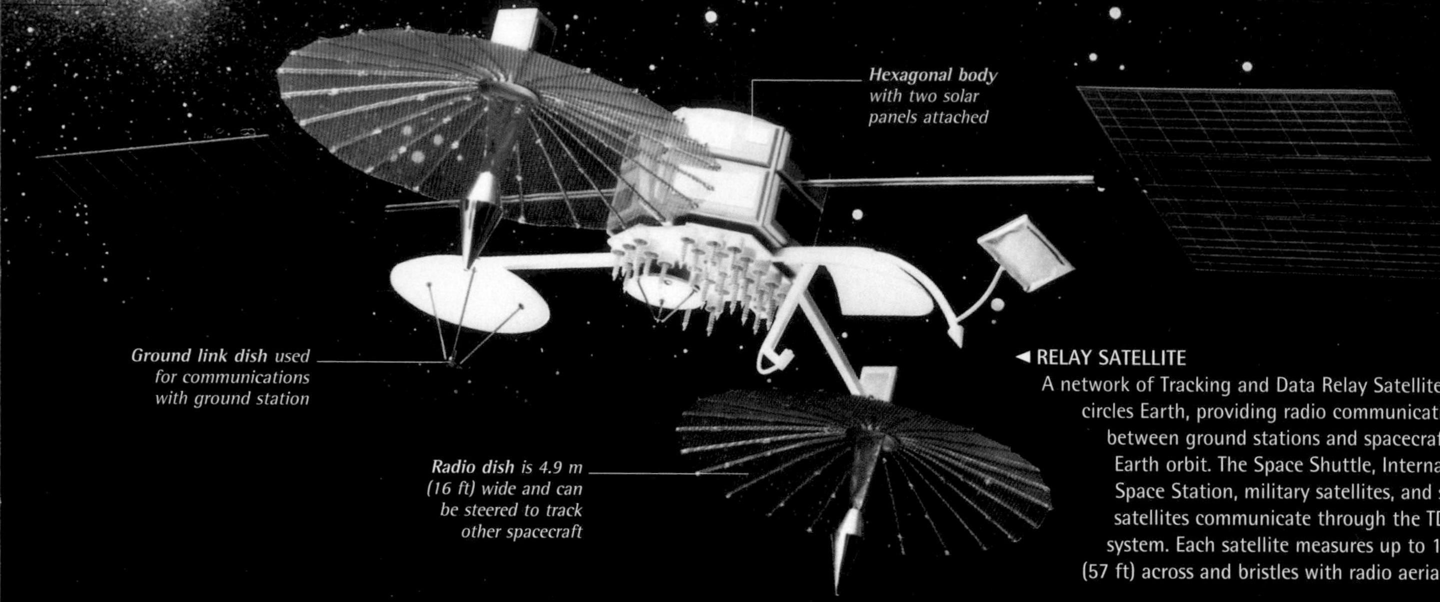

Hexagonal body
with two solar
panels attached

Ground link dish used
for communications
with ground station

Radio dish is 4.9 m
(16 ft) wide and can
be steered to track
other spacecraft

◄ RELAY SATELLITE
A network of Tracking and Data Relay Satellites (TDRS)
circles Earth, providing radio communication
between ground stations and spacecraft in
Earth orbit. The Space Shuttle, International
Space Station, military satellites, and science
satellites communicate through the TDRS
system. Each satellite measures up to 17.4 m
(57 ft) across and bristles with radio aerials.

SPACE COMMUNICATION

Reliable radio communication is vital for spaceflight.
Ground controllers need to monitor a spacecraft's
operation and transmit commands to it. They need to talk
to astronauts in manned craft and during spacewalks. In
the early days of spaceflight, ground controllers could
communicate with a spacecraft in Earth orbit only when
it was in sight of a ground station. When it disappeared
below the horizon, contact was lost. Now, a network of
satellites around the world keeps ground controllers in
constant communication with orbiting craft.

A 90-cm (3-ft)
parabolic antenna
dish operates
using microwaves

Radio
communications
system is housed in
front part of Orbiter

Communications
system is attached
to the backpack

Microphones and
earphones in
headset

Helmet contains air,
allowing astronaut to
speak into microphone
as well as breathe

◄ SPACE WALKING AND TALKING
During a spacewalk outside the Space
Shuttle Orbiter, astronauts keep in
touch by radio. The headset inside
the helmet has two microphones
and earphones. Cables from
these and from biomedical
sensors pass through the
suit to a communications
system attached to the
backpack (biomedical sensors
are small devices that monitor
the astronaut's heart beat and
other body processes). The astronaut
controls the system using switches on
the control box on the spacesuit's chest.

KEEPING IN TOUCH ▲

Astronauts on the Space Shuttle and the International Space Station can communicate with people on Earth by e-mail. They write e-mails using laptop computers and Personal Digital Assistants (PDAs) and then send them to the Johnson Space Center in Houston, Texas. Many of the messages are sent to NASA staff about the mission, but the astronauts can also send e-mails to their families. Keeping in touch with home is particularly important for astronauts on long missions.

◄ ORBITER COMMUNICATIONS

The Space Shuttle Orbiter has four separate radio communications systems. Three of them carry voice, engineering data, and science data. One of these also handles communications with astronauts outside the Orbiter. The fourth communications system is a high-bandwidth one that carries television pictures. Inside the Orbiter, astronauts connect to the communications system by plugging their headset into one of the audio terminals dotted about the crew compartment.

TWIN COMMUNICATORS ►

A ground station at White Sands, near Las Cruces, New Mexico, handles radio traffic to and from spacecraft orbiting Earth. The traffic passes to and from the spacecraft via Tracking and Data Relay satellites. The White Sands ground station houses two almost identical terminals. The system was developed because one ground station and a network of satellites provides a better service, and also costs less, than a worldwide network of ground stations.

e ▸▸

space talk

SCIENCE IN SPACE

Scientific research has been carried out in space since the very first spaceflight. Radio signals from Sputnik 1 were used to study how the atmosphere affects radio waves. Modern scientific satellites study the Earth from space and the Universe beyond. Science experiments are also carried out on manned space missions. Scientists use space experiments to remove the effect of gravity and learn more about materials, to understand living organisms better, and to study the effects of weightlessness on the human body.

Head houses a skull with a plastic brain

Radiation monitors attached to head and torso

Skin made from fire-proof material

▲ CRYSTALS GROWN IN SPACE

Crystals are used in computers, cameras, DVD players, and a variety of scientific instruments, as well as in medical research. Crystals grown on Earth are distorted by gravity – the growing crystals are pulled against the walls of their container. Crystals grown in space tend to be larger and better quality because they can spread out freely. Studying crystal growth in space is leading to ways of growing better quality crystals on Earth.

science in space

FLAMES IN SPACE ►

Flames look very different in space. Without gravity, the hot gases do not rise to form the familiar tear-drop shape of a flame on Earth. In space, a flame spreads out in all directions. As it burns more slowly and evenly, there are no colour variations. Flames have been studied in experiments carried out in the Space Shuttle. The research helps engine manufacturers who want to develop new, cleaner-burning engines. Understanding how flames behave is also important in developing ways of fighting fires in spacecraft.

FLAME ON EARTH IS ELONGATED WITH A YELLOW TIP

SPACE FLAME IS SPHERICAL AND BLUE

▲ PHANTOM TORSO

The Phantom Torso is a model of a human body used in radiation research in the International Space Station. The Earth's atmosphere blocks some of the Sun's radiation. When astronauts go into space, they lose the atmosphere's protection. Scientists are concerned about the radiation hazard. The Phantom Torso contains real bones and plastic organs packed with hundreds of sensors to measure radiation. The data produced will help scientists to predict the radiation doses humans would receive on long spaceflights.

◄ MICROGRAVITY GLOVEBOX

The International Space Station is equipped with a workstation for scientists called the Microgravity Science Glovebox. It is a sealed 255-litre (56-gallon) box where astronauts can do experiments without any risk of gases or liquids escaping into the rest of the spacecraft. Two glove-ports let astronauts reach inside and handle things without breaking the seal. Video cameras are linked to Earth so scientists here can monitor activities inside the box. The box is also equipped with its own laptop computer to control experiments and record results.

SPACELAB MISSIONS

Spacelab was an orbiting laboratory carried in the Shuttle's payload bay. There were 25 Spacelab missions, including:

Spacelab-1, 1983: 73 experiments included astronomy, life sciences, and material research

Spacelab D1, 1985: Funded by Germany, tests included botany, biology, and crystal growing

Astro 1, 1990: Ultra-violet and X-ray telescopes were used to observe the Universe

SLS 1, 1991: First Spacelab mission dedicated solely to life sciences

Spacelab J, 1992: Crew brought back the first animal embryos fertilized and developed in space

Neurolab, 1998: Last mission, it studied the effects of microgravity on the nervous system

Blacked-out
goggles minimize
distractions

Cable carries data
on the astronaut's
head position to
a computer

Tape recorder
records astronaut's
comments

Headphones block
distracting noises

▲ EXPERIMENTING ON ASTRONAUTS

Space Shuttle payload specialist Martin Fettman was spun on
a rotating chair by mission specialist Rhea Seddon to study the
effect on his balance. His headset sensed his head movements,
so they could be compared to similar experiments on Earth.
They worked inside Spacelab SLS-2, a laboratory carried in the
Shuttle's payload bay in 1993. It was one of many experiments
carried out to study the effects of weightlessness on the human
body. The whole mission was dedicated to life sciences research.

TETHERED SATELLITES ►

Satellites tethered to the Shuttle have been used to try to generate
electricity. The satellite collects data for science experiments and houses
thrusters that keep the tether tight. The action of the tether cutting
through the Earth's magnetic field produces an electric current. This
may lead to a new way of generating electricity for space stations. On
the first experiment, the tether jammed after only 256 m (840 ft) of the
20 km (12 miles) had been unreeled. On the second, it broke and the
satellite flew away!

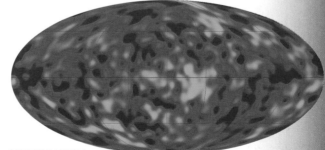

▲ EXPERIMENTS ON THE MOON

All the Apollo missions took experiments to the Moon. They
collected data about moon-quakes, magnetism, heat flow
through the surface, and the solar wind. Instruments left behind
continued to send back data for decades. Three reflectors left
were hit by laser beams fired from Earth – this helped scientists
to discover that the average distance between the centres of the
Earth and the Moon is 385,000 km (239,000 miles), and that the
Moon is receding from Earth at about 3.8 cm (1.5 in) a year.

MAPPING HEAT ▲

The Cosmic Background Explorer (COBE) satellite was launched in
1990 to map the heat given out soon after the Universe began.
This cosmic background radiation had been detected in 1965,
but COBE made a very accurate map of it. COBE's instruments
were sensitive enough to detect changes of only a few millionths
of a degree. The different colours in the map are tiny variations
in energy intensity. Scientists think these ripples became the
matter that formed the stars and galaxies.

Satellite orbits
at 23,222 km
(14,430 miles)

Navigation
antennae transmit
time signals

◄ NAVIGATION SATELLITE
The European Galileo project is a new satellite
navigation system. Navigation satellites allow
people to locate their position anywhere on Earth.
The satellites send radio signals, which are picked up
by a receiver programmed with the satellite orbits. By
calculating how far away it is from at least three satellites, the
receiver can work out its own exact position on Earth's surface. Car
navigation systems combine satellite and road map data to guide drivers.

Laser
communications
system

Antenna dish for
communicating
between satellites

Solar array
assemblage is
10 m (33 ft) long

SATELLITE DATA

Everyone uses satellite data in one way or another.
Satellites relay telephone calls, TV signals, and Internet
traffic. They provide navigation services and take
measurements of the land, sea, and atmosphere. They
map different types of rock and vegetation. Their pictures
of rainforests can reveal illegal logging. They monitor the
weather and track hurricanes so that people in their path
can be warned. Measurements of temperatures, sea
currents, and waves help scientists to
understand the oceans. Spy satellites
monitor military activity.

COMMUNICATIONS ▲
Satellites form an
essential part of the
worldwide communications
network. They relay telephone calls, including those
from mobile phones. The European Space Agency's Artemis
satellites provide navigation and communication services.
They can communicate with other satellites by laser,
allowing images of Earth taken by other satellites to be
received on Earth in as little as 30 minutes.

e ▶▶
satellites

Star tracker helps
the satellite
to navigate

Radiometer
measures sea
surface temperature

Radio antenna
transmits data
to Earth

Thermal blanket protects
against temperature
extremes

Radar altimeter
records wave
height and shape
of ocean surface

Solar array
covers 70 m²
(700 sq ft)

▲ ENVISAT
Data from the European environmental satellite,
Envisat, helps scientists to measure changes in
the environment. The satellite orbits Earth from
pole to pole, making observations of the land,
oceans, atmosphere, and ice. This photograph
shows plumes of smoke trailing away from fires
raging near the coast of Venezuela. The fires
indicate that forests are being cleared for
agriculture. Analysing data from satellites like
Envisat can help identify climate changes
caused by global warming.

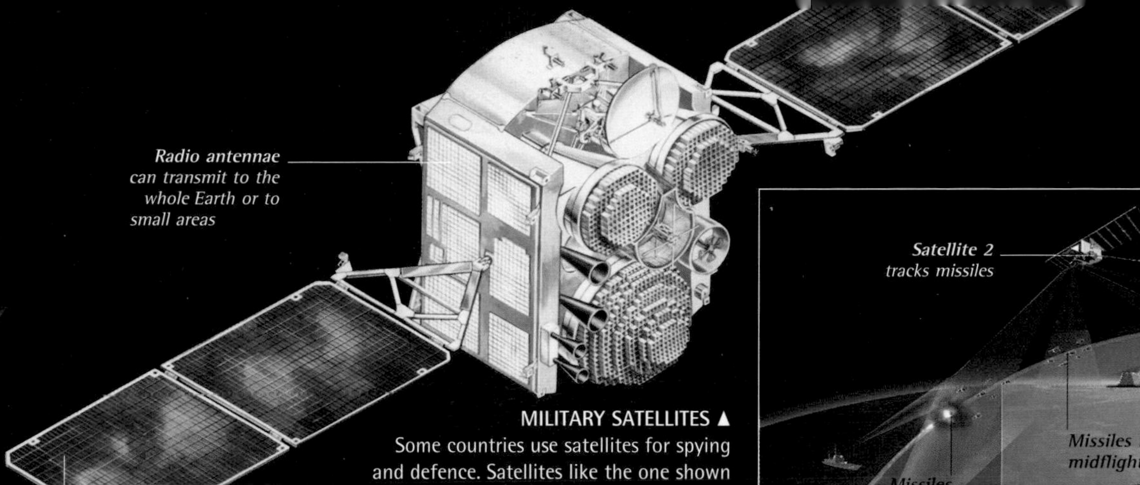

Radio antennae can transmit to the whole Earth or to small areas

Solar panel supplies electricity

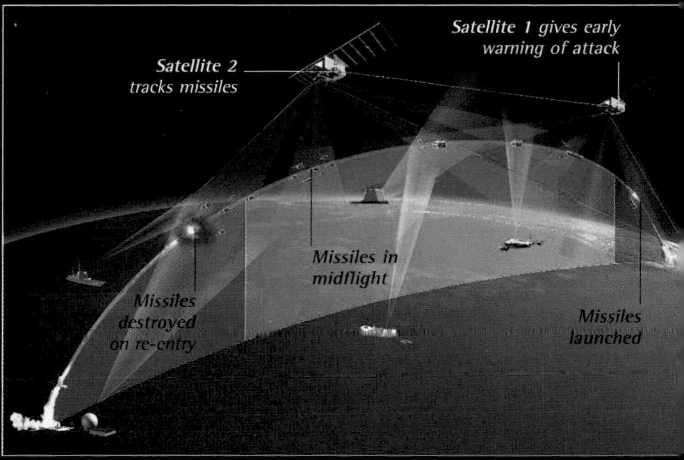

MILITARY SATELLITES ▲
Some countries use satellites for spying and defence. Satellites like the one shown above are used by US military forces for secret data communications. The US Space Tracking and Surveillance System (right) is due to start working in 2006-2007. It includes satellites that will spot missiles on launch, track their flights, and relay information to ground-based defence systems. These will destroy the missiles when they re-enter the atmosphere.

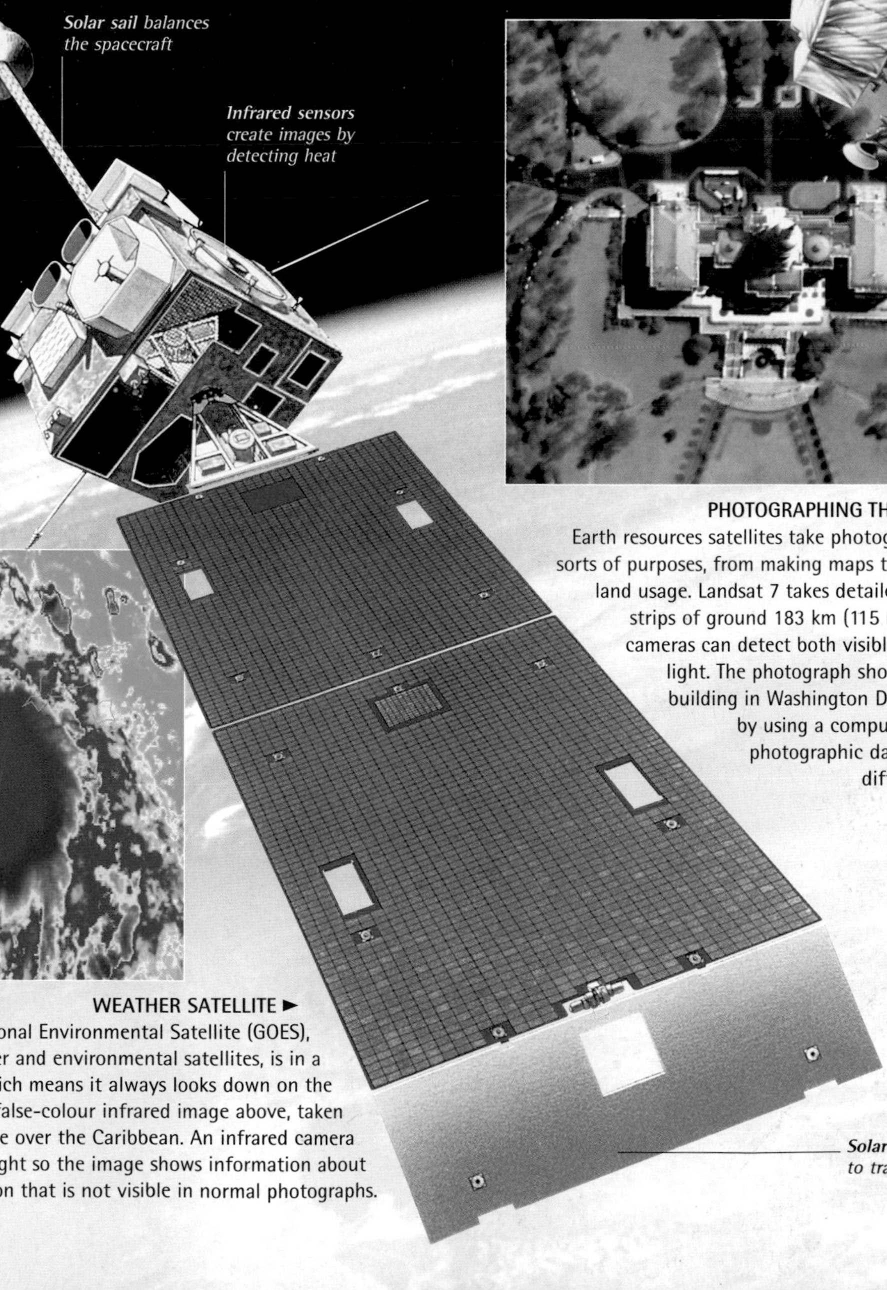

Satellite 2 tracks missiles

Satellite 1 gives early warning of attack

Missiles destroyed on re-entry

Missiles in midflight

Missiles launched

Solar sail balances the spacecraft

Infrared sensors create images by detecting heat

Payload includes cameras and infrared sensors

PHOTOGRAPHING THE PLANET ▶
Earth resources satellites take photographs for all sorts of purposes, from making maps to monitoring land usage. Landsat 7 takes detailed pictures of strips of ground 183 km (115 mile) wide. Its cameras can detect both visible and infrared light. The photograph shows the Capitol building in Washington DC. It was made by using a computer to combine photographic data from several different satellites.

Solar array provides 1.5 kw of electrical power for the satellite

WEATHER SATELLITE ▶
The Geostationary Operational Environmental Satellite (GOES), like many other weather and environmental satellites, is in a geostationary orbit, which means it always looks down on the same part of Earth. The false-colour infrared image above, taken by GOES, shows a hurricane over the Caribbean. An infrared camera detects heat rather than light so the image shows information about temperature variation that is not visible in normal photographs.

Solar array rotates to track the Sun

HUBBLE SPACE TELESCOPE

In April 1990, a telescope the size of a large bus was launched into Earth orbit. It was named the Hubble Space Telescope (HST), after the American astronomer Edwin Hubble. Soon after it was launched, astronomers found that it would not produce a sharp image. An error of just one fiftieth the width of a human hair had been made in the manufacture of the telescope's main mirror. In 1993, the Space Shuttle returned to the telescope and astronauts fixed the problem. Since then, the telescope has taken thousands of spectacular photographs of the Universe.

HUBBLE DATA	
Length: 13.2 m (44 ft)	
Diameter: 4.2 m (14 ft) (without solar arrays) 12.0 m (40 ft) (with solar arrays)	
Solar arrays: 12.0 x 2.8 m (40 x 9 ft)	
Mass: 11.1 tonnes	
Orbit: 569 km (355 miles) above Earth	
Speed: 28,000 kph (17,500 mph)	

▼ HUBBLE IN OPERATION

Light enters the narrow end of the telescope and travels down to the primary mirror. It then bounces back up to a small secondary mirror and finally passes through a hole in the primary mirror to arrive at an instrument package. This contains cameras that can photograph stars, objects in our solar system, and galaxies. One camera, the Faint Object Camera, can detect objects five times fainter than the dimmest object visible with a telescope on Earth.

Hubble

▲ COMMANDING HUBBLE

The telescope is controlled from the Space Science Institute in Baltimore, Maryland. Its flight operations team sends commands that turn it to point in the right direction. To make sharp images, it must stay pointed in one direction with extreme accuracy, equivalent to focusing on a dot the width of a human hair at a distance of 1.6 km (1 mile). Hubble operates all day, every day. It transmits enough data to fill a dozen DVDs every week.

High-gain antenna receives commands from Earth

Secondary mirror has a diameter of 30 cm (12 in)

Primary (main) mirror is 2.4 m (8 ft) in diameter

Solar array unfurls during deployment

Instrument module contains cameras and other instruments

Remote manipulator arm deploys Hubble

◄ LAUNCHING HUBBLE

The Hubble Telescope was launched on-board the Space Shuttle Discovery on 24 April 1990. The Orbiter's robot arm gently lifted it out of the payload bay. The solar arrays were designed to unfurl automatically. The first one deployed successfully, but the second one stuck. Astronauts suited up in case they would have to fix the problem, but a second attempt to deploy the array succeeded.

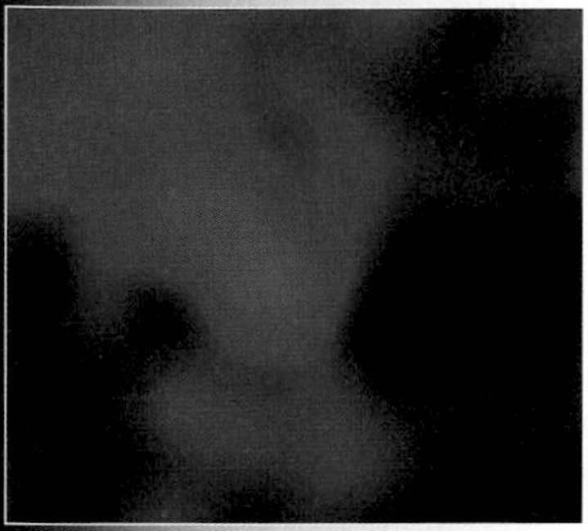

CHANDRA X-RAY IMAGE

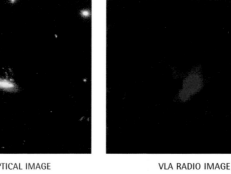

HUBBLE OPTICAL IMAGE

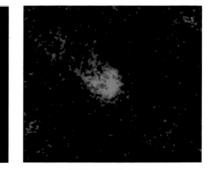

VLA RADIO IMAGE

KPNO OPTICAL IMAGE

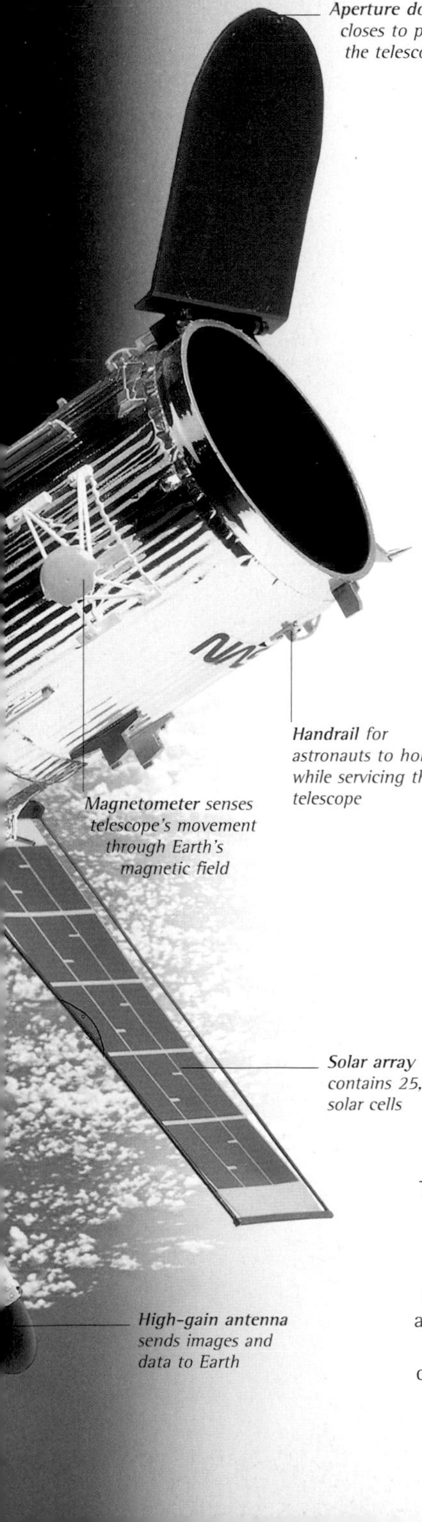

Aperture door
closes to protect
the telescope

WORKING TOGETHER ▶

Images of one object made by different types of telescope, showing different features, can be combined to form a single image. This picture was created using optical images from the Hubble Telescope and the Kitt Peak National Observatory (KPNO), an image from the group of radio telescopes called the Very Large Array (VLA), and an image from the Chandra X-ray Observatory. It shows a galaxy, called C153, being ripped apart as it races through a cluster of other galaxies at 7 million kph (4.4 million mph).

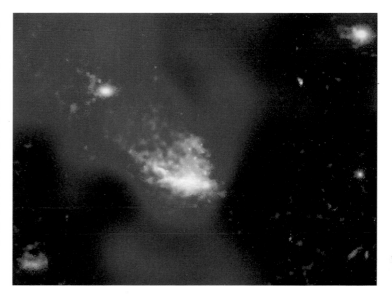

Handrail for astronauts to hold while servicing the telescope

Magnetometer senses telescope's movement through Earth's magnetic field

◀ SPITZER SPACE TELESCOPE

The Spitzer Space Telescope, formerly known as the Space Infrared Telescope Facility (SIRTF), was launched on 25 August 2003. It makes images from the heat given out by objects. It has to be in space to work, because most infrared heat rays are blocked by Earth's atmosphere. The telescope, which is 85 cm (34 in) wide, can see through clouds of dust and gas, and can reveal objects that are normally hidden from optical telescopes. It can also detect cool stars and planets orbiting other stars.

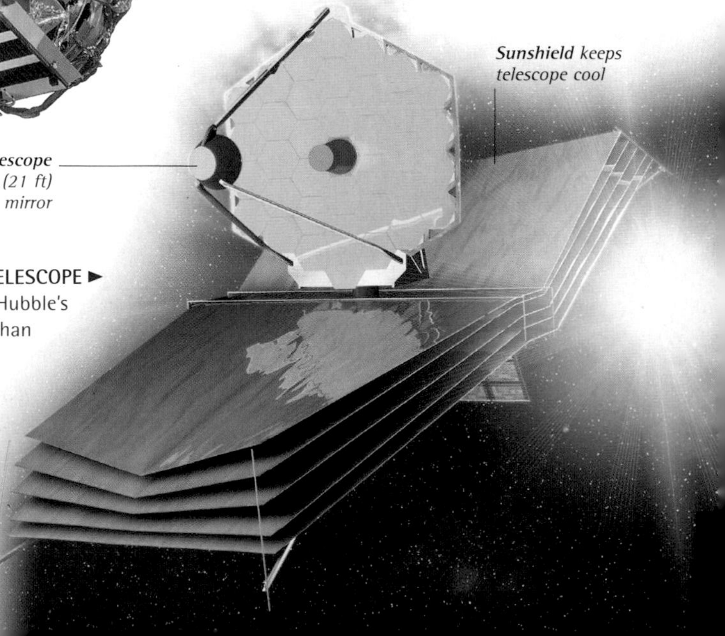

Solar array
contains 25,000
solar cells

Sunshield keeps
telescope cool

Optical telescope
with 6.5 m (21 ft)
diameter main mirror

JAMES WEBB TELESCOPE ▶

The James Webb Space Telescope (JWST) will continue Hubble's work from about the year 2011. Its mirror is more than twice the diameter of Hubble's. Large mirrors are hard to make, so the James Webb telescope's mirror is made from 18 smaller segments. It will be placed about 1.5 million km (1 million miles) from Earth. A sunshield will stop solar radiation from overheating the telescope, which will operate at a temperature of about -240°C (-400°F).

High-gain antenna
sends images and
data to Earth

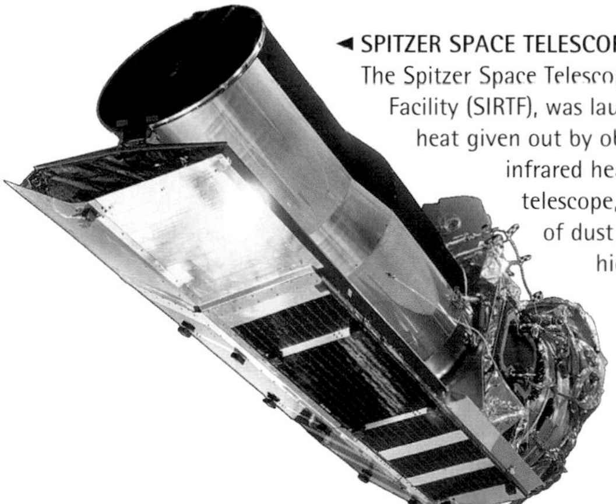

HUBBLE GALLERY

The Hubble Space Telescope has given astronomers an unimaginable view of the Universe. Some of the most beautiful images captured by the telescope show objects called planetary nebulae. These are vast clouds of gas and dust thrown off by dying stars. Hubble has also pictured colliding galaxies, jets of matter speeding through space, and some of the most distant galaxies ever seen.

Hubble

EGG NEBULA
Dust ripples outwards from an ageing star 3,000 light years away. One light year equals 9.5 million million km (5.9 million million miles), the distance light travels in a year. False colours have been added to show how light is reflected by the smoke-sized bits of dust.

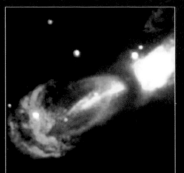

ROTTEN EGG NEBULA
The Calabash Nebula is also called the Rotten Egg, because it contains sulphur, which smells like rotten eggs!

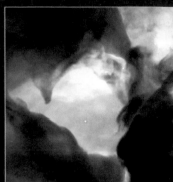

TORNADOES IN THE LAGOON NEBULA
This funnel-like structure is a pair of gas clouds spiralling around a central hot star, 5,000 light years away.

TWIN JET NEBULA
Hubble captures twin jets made from gas streaming away from a central star at 300 km (186 miles) per second.

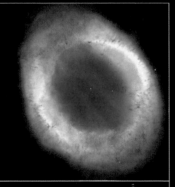

RING NEBULA
In one of the most famous planetary nebulae, the Ring Nebula, a dying star floats in a blue haze of hot gas.

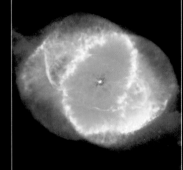

CAT'S EYE NEBULA
This 1,000-year-old planetary nebula features shells, jets, and knots of gas surrounding one or two dying stars.

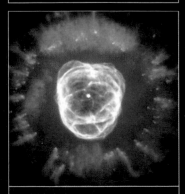

ESKIMO NEBULA
This dying sun-like star is known as the Eskimo Nebula, because it resembles a face surrounded by a fur hood.

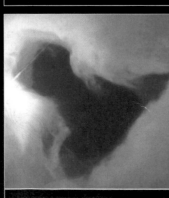

THE REFLECTION NEBULA
NGC 1999 is also called the Reflection Nebula, because dust around it reflects starlight, like fog around a street lamp.

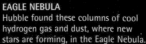

EAGLE NEBULA
Hubble found these columns of cool hydrogen gas and dust, where new stars are forming, in the Eagle Nebula.

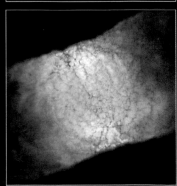

RETINA NEBULA
This rainbow of colours is a side view of a doughnut-shape of dust and gas thrown out by a dying star.

CYGNUS LOOP SUPERNOVA
Gas flies out from the explosion of a star, a supernova, 15,000 years ago. A supernova is brighter than a galaxy.

A SWARM OF ANCIENT STARS
This swarm of stars, known as NGC 6093, or M80, is one of the densest clusters in our galaxy, the Milky Way.

THE QUINTUPLET CLUSTER
Hubble zoomed in on this cluster of young stars, close to the centre of our galaxy, but hidden from Earth by dust.

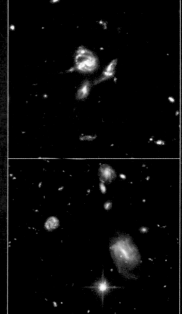

X MARKS THE BLACK HOLE
An "X" visible at the centre of nearby spiral galaxy M51 marks a black hole with a mass equal to a million Suns.

EXPANDING HALO
This shell-like shape is an expanding ball of gas and dust illuminated by a red supergiant star, V838 Monocerotis.

THE LIFE CYCLE OF STARS
The giant nebula, NGC 3603, includes stars of all ages, from newly formed stars at the centre to old supergiants.

LOOKING INTO THE PAST
These are among the oldest galaxies seen by Hubble, forming a few hundred million years after the Big Bang.

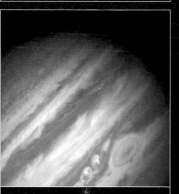

JUPITER
Hubble has taken beautiful images of the planets in our solar system. This one focuses on Jupiter's atmosphere.

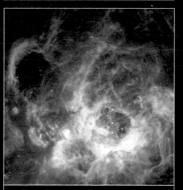

STAR FORMATION
Long streaks of gas whirling around the galaxy NGC 3079 were probably caused by a burst of star formation.

STAR NURSERY
Hubble pinpointed an area of activity in one arm of the spiral galaxy M33, a region where new stars are forming.

BIRTH OF A STAR
The dwarf galaxy, NGC 1569, is a hotbed of star formation, producing clusters of brilliant blue young stars.

SPINNING TADPOLE
The blue stars in this spiral galaxy are massive stars, 10 times hotter and a million times brighter than our Sun.

A MEETING OF GALAXIES
These two galaxies, NGC 2207 (left) and IC 2163, are spinning into each other. The stronger gravitational pull of the larger galaxy has distorted its smaller partner, sending stars and gas flying out into streamers 100,000 light years long.

A DUSTY SPIRAL
The arms of this majestic spiral galaxy are rich in clouds of dust and glowing hydrogen gas emitted by young stars.

SPACE JUNK

Wherever rockets and spacecraft go, they leave pieces of debris, or junk, behind. This space junk ranges from microscopic specks of paint and metal to whole spacecraft. Space debris is a problem, because it can collide with working satellites and manned spacecraft. Travelling at speeds of 28,000 kph (17,500 mph), even pea-sized pieces can cause serious damage. The first known collision happened in July 1996 when the French Cerise satellite collided with debris and tumbled off course. Most of the debris orbiting Earth came from exploding rockets.

space junk

▲ A NEEDLE IN THE HAYSTACK
Space junk is tracked by radar. NASA's main source of data on pieces of 1-30 cm (½-12 in) across is the Haystack X-Band radar operated by the Massachusetts Institute of Technology. It can spot an object the size of a pea more than 600 km (373 miles) away, so craft in the area can be alerted. Scanners like Haystack have shown that most debris orbits within 2,000 km (1,242 miles) of Earth, with thick bands at 800 km (497 miles), 1,000 km (621 miles), and 1,500 km (932 miles).

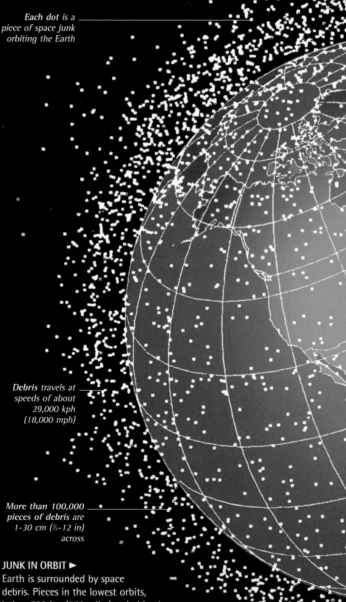

Each dot is a piece of space junk orbiting the Earth

Debris travels at speeds of about 29,000 kph (18,000 mph)

More than 100,000 pieces of debris are 1-30 cm (½-12 in) across

Moon-buggy's metal parts will not rust in space

Soft fabrics in the seats are most likely to perish

Titanium wheel treads will not corrode

▲ MOON SCRAP
The Moon is littered with junk from Earth. There are space probes that crashed or landed there before the manned landings. The descent stages of six Apollo lunar modules still stand on the surface. Three of them have had lunar rovers parked beside them since they were abandoned in the 1970s. Without air or moisture, they will not rust or rot. The only thing stopping the lunar rovers from being driven away, now or in a thousand years, is a flat battery!

JUNK IN ORBIT ►
Earth is surrounded by space debris. Pieces in the lowest orbits, below 600 km (373 miles), spiral back into the atmosphere within a few years. At a height of about 800 km (497 miles), debris can stay in orbit for decades. Debris more than 1,000 km (621 miles) above Earth may stay in orbit for a century or more. Nothing can be done about debris in orbit, but the space-faring nations have introduced guidelines to minimize orbital debris in future.

SKYLAB FALLS TO EARTH ▶

The largest pieces of junk are old space stations. When they have ended their working life, they re-enter the atmosphere. The last of three crews left the US space station Skylab on 8 February 1974. Its orbit gradually decayed (lowered) until it re-entered the atmosphere on 11 July 1979. Skylab was too big to burn up. Pieces as big as 373 kg (1,000 lb) landed in the Indian Ocean and Australia. In 2001, Russia's Mir space station shattered into 1,500 pieces, 72 km (45 miles) above Earth before landing in the Pacific Ocean.

More than 11,000 pieces of debris are 10 cm (4 in) across or larger

BEYOND THE EARTH ▶

Apollo 17's lunar module travels to the Moon, visible inside the S-IVB rocket (top). The particles surrounding it are paint and insulation flakes shed when the S-IVB, the third stage, separated from the Saturn V rocket. Once it had delivered the astronauts into orbit, the useless S-IVB was put on course to hit the Moon to test the seismometers (shock wave detectors) left there. Debris from earlier discarded spacecraft that travelled to the Moon now orbits the Sun.

◀ MICRO-TROUBLE

Microscopic particles of debris cause damage because of their high speed. This 4 mm (⅙ in) pit was made in a Space Shuttle window by a flake of paint measuring less than 0.5 mm (1/55 in)! After 15 years in space, the Mir space station was covered with dents and pits. The International Space Station is more heavily shielded than any other spacecraft, to protect it from dust and debris.

4 MM (1/6 INCH)

Energy flash on the target inside a NASA test chamber

Tens of millions of junk particles are smaller than 1 cm (½ in) across

IMPACT STUDIES ▶

This flash was produced by an object hitting a solid surface at 28,000 kph (17,500 mph). Experiments like this, at NASA's Hypervelocity Ballistics Range in California, simulate what happens to a spacecraft hit by a piece of debris. In 1985, a satellite was deliberately smashed to pieces in orbit to see what would happen to the debris. The impact produced 285 pieces, which were each tracked. By January 1998, all but eight had re-entered the atmosphere.

GOING TO THE PLANETS

Space probes have been exploring the Solar System since the early 1960s. They have flown past, orbited, crashed into, landed on, or driven across every planet except Pluto. They bristle with instruments to learn as much as possible about our planetary neighbours. Probes sent to the outer planets are also equipped with nuclear power generators, because there is too little sunlight to use solar panels. These robotic explorers have sent back thousands of stunning images and revealed many secrets.

Mariner 10 revealed Mercury's crater-scarred surface

▲ MARINER REACHES MERCURY

Mariner 10 gave scientists their first close-up view of Mercury. Launched in 1973, it was the first probe to visit two planets. The gravitational pull of Venus was used to swing the 503 kg (1,109 lb) probe around and propel it towards Mercury. Mariner 10 was the first probe to use this manoeuvre, called gravity assist. Between 1974 and 1975, it flew within 271 km (146 miles) of Mercury, three times, taking 2,800 photographs.

Odyssey took thermal images of Mars to show scientists its mineral content

◄ MARS

Mars has fascinated people for generations. In 1965, Mariner 4 took photographs looking for signs of life, but found none. Two Viking probes landed in 1976 and tested soil, but the results weren't clear. A tiny rover called Sojourner landed in 1997, sending back 550 images. In 2001, Odyssey entered Mars' orbit to study climate and geology. In 2004, two larger rovers, Spirit and Opportunity, landed. Other probes have mapped its surface, still searching for life-forms.

Galileo photographed Jupiter and its moons, including Europa

◄ JUPITER

Jupiter is the Solar System's biggest planet. More than 1,300 Earths would fit inside it. A vast storm, called the Great Red Spot, has been raging there for the past 300 years. Pioneer 10 took the first close-up pictures of Jupiter in 1973. Pioneer 11 and two Voyager probes followed. In 1995, after a six-year flight, Galileo went into orbit around Jupiter and dropped a mini-probe into its atmosphere. It found that the gas giant is mostly hydrogen.

VENUS ►

Radar data collected by a series of probes, including Pioneer Venus and Magellan, was used to make this false-colour image of Venus. The planet is hidden beneath a thick, poisonous atmosphere, but radar can see through it and map the surface. Computers use the data to create 3-D views (far right). The Soviet Venera 3 probe was the first to land on Venus in 1965.

PLUTO

◄ SEEING SATURN

Saturn is the Solar System's most beautiful
planet, with its broad flat rings made of pieces
of rock and ice. This false-colour photograph shows
bands of clouds in the atmosphere. Launched in 1973,
Pioneer 11 followed its twin probe Pioneer 10 across the asteroid
belt. After visiting Jupiter, it reached Saturn in 1979 and located two
undiscovered moons and another ring. Both Pioneer probes have now left our
Solar System. Voyagers 1 and 2 visited Saturn in the early 1980s. The Cassini
space probe arrived in 2004. Cassini carries a mini-probe, called Huygens. It is
designed to explore Titan, one of Saturn's moons, which may have liquid oceans.

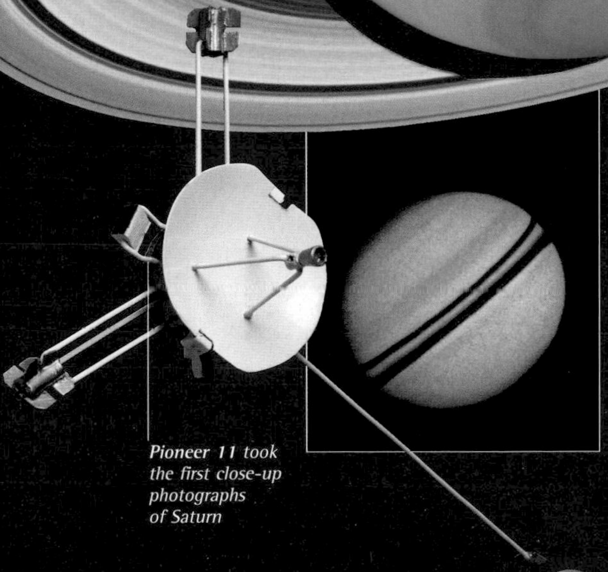

*Pioneer 11 took
the first close-up
photographs
of Saturn*

VOYAGE TO URANUS ►

This false-colour picture shows Uranus's rings, discovered
in 1977. Uranus is an odd planet. It is tipped over on
its side and spins in the opposite direction to Earth.
When Voyager 2, the only probe to visit Uranus,
arrived in 1986, its south pole pointed straight at
the Sun. The probe also discovered ten previously
unknown moons. Uranus is a gas giant, like
Jupiter and Saturn. It is covered by a hazy
blue-green atmosphere made from
hydrogen, helium, and methane.

*A radar image of Venus with
different colours representing
heights on the surface*

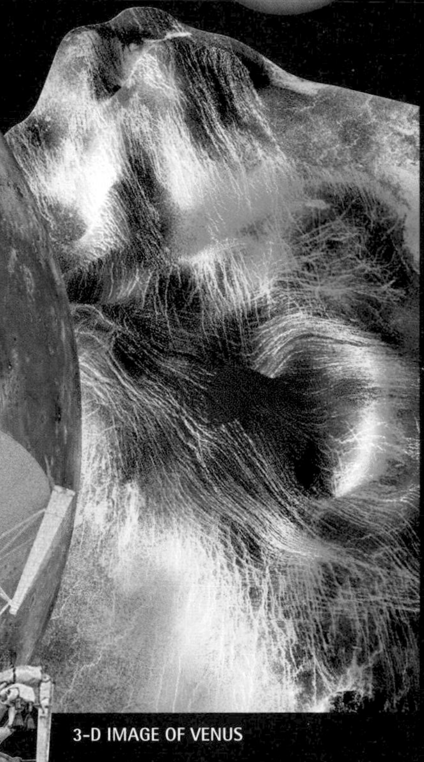

probes

*Voyager 2 confirmed the
existence of Uranus's rings
(above) then went on to Neptune*

NEPTUNE ▼

Neptune is the furthest gas planet from the Sun. Only tiny Pluto is
further away. When Voyager 2 arrived in 1989, it photographed
a giant storm (below), nicknamed the Great Dark Spot.
When the Hubble photographed Neptune in 1996, the
storm had disappeared. Neptune has the fastest winds
in the Solar System at 2,500 kph (1,350 mph). Like
Jupiter, Saturn, and Uranus, it also has rings.

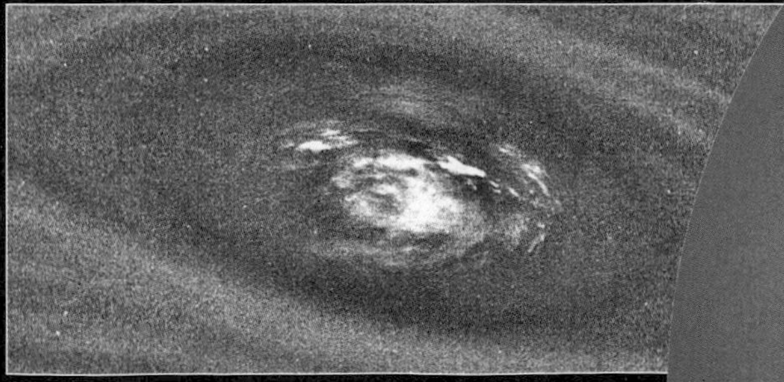

3-D IMAGE OF VENUS

*Magellan, built from
leftover parts of other
spacecraft, reached
Venus in 1990*

USA

MARS MISSION

Two Mars Exploration Rovers (MER), called Spirit and Opportunity, landed on opposite sides of Mars in January 2004. As part of NASA's long-term Mars Exploration Program, their main aim was to seek evidence for the existence of water on Mars in the past. Spirit touched down in Gusev Crater and Opportunity landed in the Meridiani Planum. The landing sites were chosen because Gusev Crater may once have been a lake and Meridiani Planum has minerals that are normally associated with water.

ACIDALIA PLANITIA

METEORITE IMPACT CRATERS

LUNAE PLANUM   GANGES CHASMA

VALLES MARINERIS GIANT CANYON SYSTEM

SOLIS PLANUM

SWIRLING DUST STORM

RADIATION LEVELS ON MARS

These maps show radiation levels all over Mars. They are hundreds of times higher than on Earth. Astronauts should be able to survive a mission to Mars, but for now it is safer to send robots to explore.

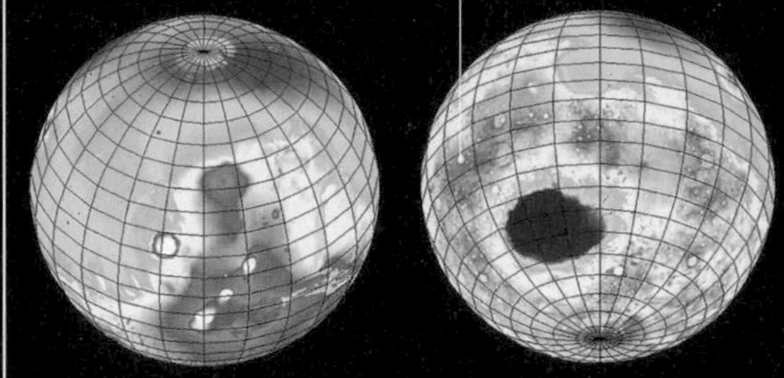

False-colour map highlights radiation levels

In the USA, the annual radiation dose is 150 millirem (1.5 millisievert) at sea level. Millirems and millisieverts are units of radiation dose.

KEY: *annual radiation dose on Mars*

| 20 rem/year | 22 | 24 | 26 | 28 | 30 |

◄ HOSTILE ENVIRONMENT

Mars is the most Earth-like of all the planets. It has polar ice caps, an atmosphere, weather, and seasons, but it is still a very hostile environment compared to Earth. The Martian atmosphere is 100 times thinner than Earth's and made mainly from carbon dioxide. The Viking spacecraft that landed there in 1976 recorded night temperatures as low as -100°C (-148°F). The surface is dry and dusty. Winds sometimes whip up the fine dust into sand-storms that can rage at 400 kph (249 mph).

◄ EVIDENCE OF WATER?

Opportunity took this false-colour photograph of a rock outcrop on Mars in an area called Shoemaker's Patio. It shows finely layered sediments, giving the rocks a striped appearance. Tiny round grains, nicknamed blueberries, are spread all over the rocks. These features, or concretions, are known to form in wet conditions. They may be strong evidence pointing to the existence of water in the past.

MARS DATA

Diameter at equator:	6,794 km (4,222 miles)
Average distance from Sun:	227.9 million km (141.6 million miles)
Year (time to orbit Sun):	687 days
Day (time to spin once):	24.62 hours
Mass:	0.11 x Earth's
Gravity:	0.38 x Earth's
Average temperature:	-63°C (-81°F)
Moons:	2 (Phobos and Deimos)

▲ RUSTY RED PLANET

This panoramic picture shows the part of the planet where the Spirit rover landed. Mars' dusty surface is red because it contains a lot of iron chemically combined with oxygen – rust! The shallow depression on the left of the rock-strewn area is a 200 m (656 ft) crater called Bonneville. The crater was probably caused by a massive meteorite slamming into the Martian surface. Mars has been repeatedly hit by meteorites, leaving a layer of debris over it.

LANDING ROVERS ON MARS

PLUNGING TO THE PLANET
The lander enters the atmosphere at nearly 20,000 kph (12,428 mph). Friction between the craft and the atmosphere heats it to 1,450°C (2,642°F). The atmosphere acts like a brake and slows the craft down.

RETRO-FIRE
About 9,000 m (29,526 ft) above Mars, a parachute is deployed. Twenty seconds later, the heat shield falls away. Air bags inflate to protect the lander. Then rockets fire and bring it to a halt 10 m (33 ft) above the surface.

TOUCHDOWN
The lander is released from the parachute and falls to the surface. It bounces and rolls for up to a kilometre (nearly a mile) before it comes to a halt. Then it transmits its first radio signal to Earth to announce its arrival.

DRIVING AWAY
The air bags are deflated and the lander opens up to form a platform and ramps. The lander unfolds its solar panels to generate electricity. Then it is carefully steered down one of the ramps and onto the Martian surface.

MARS ROVER ►
The robotic geologists, Spirit and Opportunity, stand 1.5 m (5 ft) high and weigh 185 kg (408 lb). Six wheels powered by electric motors take them roving over Mars, and they are equipped with cameras and instruments to find interesting rocks and analyse them. Soon after each sunrise, they receive commands from Earth and work until sunset. Data collected by the two robotic explorers, including images, is transmitted directly to Earth via the Deep Space Network, or to a spacecraft orbiting Mars.

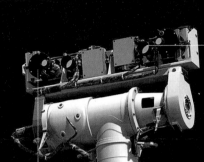

Navigation cameras provide a view of the terrain to help NASA scientists plan the rover's movements

Panoramic cameras take high-resolution, wide-angle pictures of the Martian surfaces

Pancam mast assembly (PMA) supports panoramic and navigation cameras and rotates 360° to view in different directions

Low gain aerial for radio communications

High gain aerial relays findings to a Mars-orbiting spacecraft or to NASA's Deep Space Network (DSN)

Mars

Solar panels generate electricity from sunlight

Robotic arm carries a rock abrasion tool to grind rock samples and a microscopic imager to view them in close-up

Two spectrometers analyse rocks

Rocker-bogie mobility system for scrambling over rocky terrain

ASTEROID ALERT

The Solar System formed from a cloud of gas and dust that collapsed in on itself about 4.5 billion years ago. Clumps of matter in the cloud attracted more matter onto them. The clumps collided and joined together, making bigger objects and eventually forming the planets. Asteroids are chunks of rock that did not form into planets and have survived to the present day. Most orbit the Sun between Mars and Jupiter, but collisions occasionally send one into a new orbit that may bring it closer to Earth, posing a risk of a disastrous impact.

DACTYL

IDA

◄ ASTEROID AND MOON
Asteroids are smaller than planets and exert a much weaker gravitational pull. Even so, asteroids can attract small objects towards them. In 1993, as the Galileo space probe made its way to Jupiter, it passed an asteroid called Ida. Ida is about 58 km (36 miles) long, and its cratered surface suggests that it is about one billion years old. Galileo's photographs revealed that Ida has a companion. It is being orbited by its own tiny moon, called Dactyl.

Communication antenna is 1.5 m (6 ft) in diameter

Solar arrays generate 1.8 kW of electrical power

NEAR SHOEMAKER PROBE

LANDING ON AN ASTEROID ►
The Near Earth Asteroid Rendezvous (NEAR) was the first space mission designed solely to study an asteroid. In February 2000, the NEAR Shoemaker probe approached an asteroid called 433 Eros. Ground controllers manoeuvred the spacecraft into orbit around the asteroid. After a year in orbit, photographing Eros from as little as 5 km (3 miles) away, the spacecraft was commanded to land on the asteroid in February 2001.

Thruster used to steer probe

5 KM (3 MILES)

METEORITES ►
Billions of pieces of rock, most as small as grains of sand, enter Earth's atmosphere from space every day. Most burn up in a streak of light called a meteor, or shooting star. Meteorites are larger rocks that reach the ground. Most meteorites are made of rock. A few are made of iron or a mixture of rock and iron. Some meteorites originated from the Moon or Mars, but (like asteroids) most consist of material from the early Solar System.

▲ IMPACT CRATER
Asteroids have hit Earth in the past. This crater in Arizona was caused 50,000 years ago by the impact of an asteroid that was roughly 45 m (150 ft) across. Known as the Barringer crater, it is 1.2 km (¾ mile) wide and 200 m (658 ft) deep. An even bigger object, which may have been an asteroid or a comet, struck Earth off the coast of Mexico 65 million years ago and is thought to have hastened the extinction of the dinosaurs.

▲ THE TUNGUSKA EVENT
In 1908, a huge explosion was traced to the Tunguska River region of Siberia. Scientists who investigated found an amazing sight. Whole forests had been flattened up to 30 km (19 miles) away from the impact point. There was no crater, so the object probably exploded in mid-air. Scientists reckon it must have been a comet or an asteroid made of loosely bound material. It weighed up to one million tonnes.

EFFECTS OF ASTEROIDS HITTING EARTH

SIZE OF ASTEROID	POSSIBLE DAMAGE
50 m (165 ft)	Most of the asteroid would burn up or explode in the atmosphere. The remainder would be slowed down so much that it could do little damage outside the impact site.
50–100 m (165–330 ft)	Cities the size of Greater London, Tokyo, or New York could be destroyed. Hundreds of square kilometres of land would be devastated and forests flattened.
1 km (3,300 ft)	Enough dust would be thrown up into the atmosphere to reduce temperatures and dim sunlight around the world, causing environmental damage in most countries. Up to 1.5 billion people could be killed.
10 km (6 miles)	The impact would cause earthquakes worldwide. Red-hot ash thrown up into the atmosphere would cause widespread fires as it rained down. Chemicals released by the impact would destroy the ozone layer and cause acid rain. So much dust would be thrown up that temperatures would fall and sunlight would be dimmed enough to kill crops all over the world. Most of the human race would die.

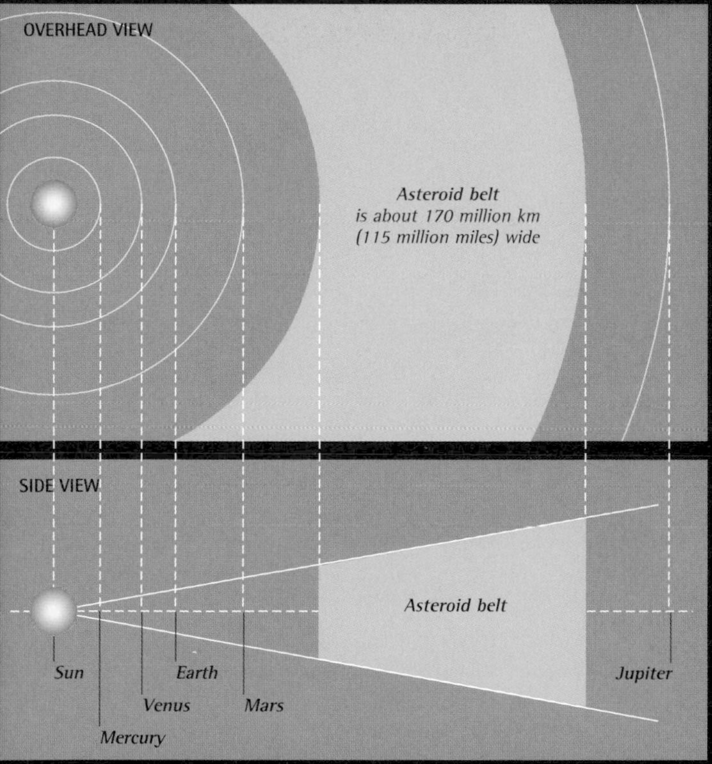

OVERHEAD VIEW

Asteroid belt
is about 170 million km
(115 million miles) wide

SIDE VIEW

Asteroid belt

Sun   Earth   Jupiter
        Venus   Mars
   Mercury

▲ THE ASTEROID BELT

Most asteroids orbit the Sun in a broad band called the asteroid belt, which is situated between the orbits of Mars and Jupiter. The belt extends from about 330 million km to almost 500 million km (185 to 300 million miles) from the Sun. There are also two groups of asteroids in the same orbit as Jupiter. Known as the Trojans, one group orbits the Sun ahead of Jupiter and another group follows the giant planet.

e ▶▶

asteroids

ROCKS IN SPACE ▶

Asteroids range in size from large boulders to rocks hundreds of kilometres across. Most are lumpy, not spherical like planets, because their gravity is too weak to pull them into a round shape. The largest, Ceres, was the first to be discovered, in 1801. Ceres is 940 km (584 miles) wide and orbits at an average of 415 million km (258 million miles) from the Sun. It contains one-third of the total mass of all asteroids in the Solar System.

Tails always point away from the Sun

Dust tail can be up to 10 million km long

Gas tail can be hundreds of km long

Head is a solid nucleus surrounded by a coma of gas and dust

ORBITING A COMET ►
The Rosetta spacecraft will orbit Comet 67P/Churyumov-Gerasimenko after a ten-year journey through space. The comet was discovered in 1969. The 4-km (2.5-mile) wide ball of ice and dust is travelling at 136,000 kph (85,000 mph). Manoeuvring the spacecraft into orbit around the comet is very tricky, because the spacecraft's flight path is affected by dust and jets of gas coming from the comet, and also by its weak and irregular gravity.

◄ INSIDE A COMET
Hale-Bopp was the brightest comet for over 20 years when it passed the Sun in 1997. Millions of people on Earth saw it. Most comets are less than 15 km (10 miles) across. Hale-Bopp's nucleus, the solid part in the middle, is 40 km (25 miles) across. As it neared the Sun, it developed two tails – a yellow dust tail and a blue gas tail. It passed within 138 million km (86 million miles) of the Sun on 1 April 1997. Hale-Bopp will return in 2,392 years.

GIOTTO

In 1986, a European spacecraft called Giotto met up with the most famous comet of all, Halley's Comet, and took close-up photographs of it. The comet is named after English astronomer Edmond Halley (1656-1742). He realized that comets seen in 1531, 1607, and 1682 were the same comet returning every 76 years. He predicted it would return in 1758. He was right.

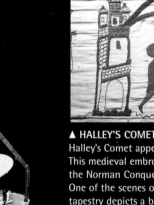

▲ HALLEY'S COMET IN 1066...
Halley's Comet appears on the Bayeux Tapestry. This medieval embroidery shows the story of the Norman Conquest of England in 1066. One of the scenes on the 70-m (229-ft) long tapestry depicts a bright star with a long fiery tail. Calculations have shown that this is actually Halley's Comet. The comet is also portrayed in a fresco on the birth of Christ by Italian artist Giotto di Bondone, painted in 1304. In fact, appearances of Halley's Comet have been recorded all the way back to 240 BC.

▲ ...AND TODAY
Halley's Comet is still making its regular appearances today. The 16-km long (10½-mile) chunk of rock and ice made its latest appearance in 1986. It passed within about 88 million km (55 million miles) of the Sun. It is expected to return in the year 2061. Some comets have much shorter or longer orbits than Halley. Comet Encke returns every 3.3 years, while Comet Hyakutake, last seen in 1996, will probably not return for another 14,000 years.

ROSETTA'S COMET ENCOUNTER

ORBITER
Rosetta will be the first craft to orbit a comet, one of the most difficult manoeuvres ever attempted. It will be the first to accompany a comet as it travels towards the Sun. It will study the comet for nearly two years, and carries a craft that will land on the surface of the comet's nucleus.

LANDER
The orbiter has to be guided with precision to ensure that the lander is ejected in the right direction to land on the comet's nucleus. As the lander touches down, it anchors itself on the surface by firing two harpoons into the nucleus. Its legs automatically adjust themselves to keep upright.

EXPERIMENTS
The lander will analyse the chemical composition of the comet's surface and drill into the nucleus to analyse material from below the surface. It will also test the strength of the surface, its texture, ice content, and how porous it is. Data will be transmitted to Rosetta to relay back to Earth.

Navigation cameras help to keep the craft on course

Cameras take high-resolution images of the comet's nucleus

Radio aerial uses radio waves to study the comet's orbit

The CONSERT experiment will probe the comet with radio signals

Solar panels, 14 m (45 ft) long, rotate to face the Sun

Philae, the 100-kg (220-lb) lander, will land on the comet's nucleus

comets

ROSETTA MISSION SCHEDULE

PLANNED PHASE	PREDICTED DATE
Rosetta launched by Ariane 5	March 2004
First Earth gravity assist	March 2005
Mars gravity assist	March 2007
Second Earth gravity assist	November 2007
Third Earth gravity assist	November 2009
Rosetta enters hibernation	July 2011
End of hibernation	January 2014
Rendezvous with comet	May 2014
Global mapping	August 2014
Lander delivery	November 2014
Perihelion (closest to Sun)	August 2015
End of mission	December 2015

Steerable high gain radio dish, 2.2 m (7 ft) wide, is used for communication with Earth

▲ ROSETTA SPACECRAFT
Rosetta's flight path to Comet Churyumov-Gerasimenko takes it around Earth three times and Mars once, using the planets' gravity to swing it round onto the right course. The spacecraft has a cube-shaped body measuring 2.8 m by 2.1 m by 2.0 m (10 ft by 7 ft by 6 ft 6 in), and weighs 3,000 kg (6,614 lb). More than half of this is propellant. The scientific package, carrying 20 scientific instruments, weighs only 165 kg (363 lb).

SATURN'S RINGS

Saturn is the sixth planet from the Sun. It is encircled by a broad band of rings. These were a mystery when astronomers saw them for the first time in the early 1600s. They are still not fully understood, even though they have now been studied by telescopes and space probes. In 2004, the Cassini space probe arrived at Saturn to study the giant gas planet and its rings and moons. It carried a mini-probe, called Huygens, to investigate Saturn's largest moon, Titan. Scientists think that the air in Titan's atmosphere is similar to the air that existed on Earth billions of years ago.

Five instruments analyse Titan's atmosphere

Gold foil insulates and protects instruments

▲ HUYGENS

The 318-kg (700-lb) Huygens probe enters Titan's atmosphere at 21,600 kph (13,500 mph). The atmosphere slows it to 1,440 kph (900 mph), then it descends to the surface by parachute. In the two hours it takes to reach the surface, its camera takes more than 1,100 images. On-board instruments sample the atmosphere and radio their results to the Cassini spacecraft. The probe is named after Dutch astronomer Christiaan Huygens (1629-1695), who discovered Titan.

CASSINI-HUYGENS ►

Cassini-Huygens is a joint NASA-ESA mission. ESA's contribution is the Huygens probe. The Cassini spacecraft, named after the Italian astronomer Giovanni Cassini who first spotted and charted Saturn's moons, is touring the Saturn system for four years. The tour includes 74 orbits of Saturn, 44 fly-bys of its largest moon, Titan, and numerous fly-bys of Saturn's other moons. The spacecraft is powered by three nuclear electricity generators. Its science package includes instruments designed to study Saturn's gravity and its magnetic field. It also carries a digital imaging system to photograph Saturn and its moons.

Boom carries instruments to measure Saturn's magnetic field

High-gain radio dish is 4 m (13 ft) in diameter

Saturn

PLANETS WITH RINGS

JUPITER
Saturn is not the only planet with rings. All the giant gas planets (Jupiter, Saturn, Uranus, and Neptune) have rings, although none is as visible or complex as Saturn's. Voyager 2 photographed this faint ring system around Jupiter in 1999.

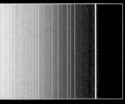

URANUS
Voyager 2 photographed rings around Uranus in 1986. This false-colour image was taken from a distance of 4.2 million km (2.6 million miles). Astronomers discovered them in 1977 when they noticed that a star dimmed as it passed behind each ring.

NEPTUNE
Neptune's rings, photographed by Voyager 2 in 1979, are so faint that they are invisible from Earth. The darkest parts of the rings dimmed starlight passing through them, but astronomers were not sure if they were rings until Voyager visited Neptune.

SATURN'S RINGS ►
Saturn's rings are made from billions of chunks of ice and rock of all sizes. The rings are very broad, but also extremely thin. As seen from Earth, they are about 275,000 km (168,000 miles) across, but their overall diameter is around 415,000 km (258,000 miles). They are perhaps only about 100 m (328 ft) thick. No one knows where the rings came from. They may be the remains of comets, asteroids, or moons that were smashed apart by collisions.

Pan · Atlas · Prometheus · Janus · Pandora · Epimetheus · Mimas · Enceladus · Telesto · Calypso · Tethys · Helene · Dione · Rhea · Titan · Hyperion · Iapetus · Phoebe

SATURN'S MOONS ▲

Until 1977, astronomers had spotted nine moons orbiting Saturn.
Since then, the Hubble Space Telescope and space probes have found
more. Pioneer 11, Voyager 1, and Voyager 2 flew past Saturn between 1979
and 1981. By the time the Cassini space probe approached Saturn in 2004, the
number of discovered moons had risen to 31. Saturn's largest moon,
Titan, is bigger than the planets Mercury and Pluto. As a moon,
it is second in size only to Jupiter's moon, Ganymede.

SATURN ▶

Saturn is the solar system's second biggest planet.
About 746 Earths would fit inside it. For such a big
planet, it spins remarkably quickly. It rotates about
once every 10 hours – more than twice as fast as
tiny Earth. It orbits the Sun nearly 10 times
further out than the Earth and takes 29.5 years
to circle it. Saturn is the only planet that is
less dense than water. If you could find a big
enough pool, Saturn would float in it.

*Two identical engines
are fitted – one is used,
the other is a back-up*

*Rings are composed of
about 1,000 ringlets*

*Huygens probe
travels inside this
dish-shaped aeroshell*

LOOKING CLOSER AT THE RINGS

BRAIDING
The Voyager 2 probe took
pictures of a ring (called the
F ring) twisting around itself.
Scientists call it braiding. They
think the braiding is caused by
the gravity of two tiny moons,
Pandora and Prometheus.

MOON EFFECTS
Saturn's many moons exert an
influence on the rings. The
gravitational pull of each
moon attracts billions of ring
particles. This may be the
reason for some of the gaps
and fine details in the rings.

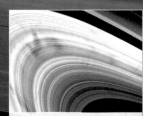

SPOKES
Scientists are puzzled by dark
lines on the rings, like spokes
on a wheel. They are thought
to be fine dust raised above
the rings by an electrostatic
effect (electrically charged
particles being forced apart).

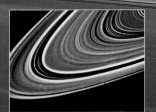

COLOUR
Photographing the rings
through coloured filters shows
extra detail. This Voyager 2
image is composed of frames
taken through clear, orange,
and ultraviolet filters from 8.9
million km (5.5 million miles).

DEEP SPACE NETWORK

NASA's Deep Space Network is responsible for tracking, commanding, and receiving data from space probes throughout the solar system. Some of the spacecraft are so far away and they use such small transmitters, that radio signals received from them are about 20 million times weaker than a watch battery. To receive such weak signals, the Deep Space Network uses huge dish-shaped antennae up to 70 m (230 ft) across. To dispatch commands to the most remote spacecraft, the same giant dishes are used to send radio signals from immensely powerful, 400-kilowatt transmitters.

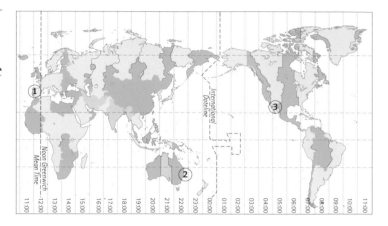

▲ DISH LOCATIONS
The Deep Space Network's antennae are located at three sites: **1** Madrid, Spain, **2** Canberra, Australia, and **3** California, USA. The sites were chosen because they are roughly 120 degrees, one third of the way round the world, from each other. As the Earth turns, at least one of the stations is always in contact with a space probe. This ensures a 24-hour observation, with overlapping time to transfer the radio link to the next station. The sites are also surrounded by mountains, which shield them from radio interference. The map shows the time difference between the three countries.

Deep Space Network

▼ DISHES IN THE DESERT
The American part of the Deep Space Network is the Goldstone Complex, 72 km (45 miles) northeast of Barstow, in the Mojave Desert in California. Goldstone is the centre of the Deep Space Network and it has the most dishes. In addition to the big 70-m (230-ft) dish, it also has six 34-m (112-ft) dishes and one 26-m (85-ft) dish. The first spacecraft it communicated with were the interplanetary space probes Pioneer 3 in 1958 and Pioneer 4 in 1959.

FROM SPACE TO SPAIN ►
The Spanish Deep Space Network complex is located near the village of Robledo de Chavela, 56 km (35 miles) west of Madrid. It became operational in 1965, replacing an earlier ground station near Johannesburg, South Africa. A new 34-m (112-ft) dish was built at the Madrid complex at the end of 2003 to add another 70 hours of tracking time per week. The increase in capacity was necessary because of the large number of space probes exploring the solar system.

AUSTRALIAN ARRAYS ►
The Australian complex was first used in 1964 and participated in the Mariner 4 mission to Mars. It is located in the Tidbinbilla Valley, 35 km (22 miles) southwest of Canberra. The 64-m (98-ft) Parkes radio dish, named after the nearby town of Parkes, also handles Deep Space Network communications. It was linked to the Canberra and Goldstone dishes to receive signals from the Galileo spacecraft, a technique called arraying.

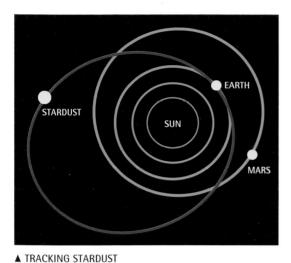

▲ TRACKING STARDUST

One of the missions being tracked by the Deep Space Network is the Stardust mission to collect particles of dust from a comet and return them to Earth. The Stardust spacecraft was launched on 7 February 1999, and it will return to Earth with its precious samples in 2006. The Deep Space Network will track Stardust during its journey to Comet Wild-2 and back, send the command signals to keep it on course, and receive the data it sends back.

DATA ON THE DEEP SPACE NETWORK

Tracking distance: A 70-m (230-ft) dish is capable of tracking a spacecraft more than 16 billion km (10 million miles) from Earth

Tracking time: The radio signal from Voyager 1 takes 12 hours and 39 minutes to reach Earth

DSN power: Transmitter power needed to command a distant probe is 400,000 watts

Probe power: Typical space probe transmitter power is 20 watts

Power from probe: Power recieved on Earth from distant space probe is one billionth of one trillionth of one watt

Most distant probe: Voyager 1 is 13.6 billion km (8.5 billion miles) from the Sun

Gas and dust trail from Comet Wild-2

High-gain antenna sends data to Earth

STARDUST'S DISCOVERIES ▶

On 2 January 2004, after a journey of 3.2 billion km (2 billion miles), the Stardust probe successfully flew through the gas and dust coma around the nucleus of Comet Wild-2 and collected dust samples. It came within 240 km (150 miles) of the icy nucleus and took the most detailed close-up pictures of a comet ever captured by a spacecraft. The images received by the Deep Space Network show what looks like a pock-marked rock 5 km (3 miles) across, with dust and gas jets streaming from its surface.

LONG-DISTANCE PHOTOGRAPHY

RAW DATA FROM THE PROBE
When a spacecraft camera takes a picture, light from the object strikes a microchip called a CCD (Charge-Coupled Device). The chip's surface is divided into a grid of hundreds of thousands of light-sensitive picture elements, or pixels. The brightness of each pixel is changed into a number, from 0 (black) to 255 (white). The same view is also photographed through colour filters. Then all the numbers are converted to digital code and transmitted to Earth.

FORMING AN IMAGE
The stream of digital data from a spacecraft is received by the Deep Space Network and relayed to the Jet Propulsion Laboratory (JPL) in Pasadena, California. JPL's computers form the data into a series of lines. They change the digital code back into numbers, and the numbers into spots of light of the right level of brightness. The black and white pictures taken through coloured filters are also combined to form false-colour images.

PROCESSING PICTURES
The first pictures created often have faults where data had become corrupted or is missing. The pictures are processed by computer to improve their quality by removing faults and unwanted noise (background data). Ultraviolet, infra-red, and radar data from space probes are processed to make pictures too, by giving false colours to the different numbers in the data. False-colour images show information that is normally invisible, such as heat, speed, or height.

SEARCHING FOR LIFE

The Universe is so vast that many astronomers think it is unlikely that Earth is the only planet hosting life. The outer planets were thought to be too cold and dark. Then the discovery of creatures in the cold, dark world at the bottom of Earth's oceans showed that life could exist in such conditions. Scientists look for signs of life in the Solar System by analysing images and soil samples sent back by probes. They also look for intelligent life in the Universe by searching for radio signals that intelligent beings might have sent. The work is called SETI, the search for extraterrestrial intelligence.

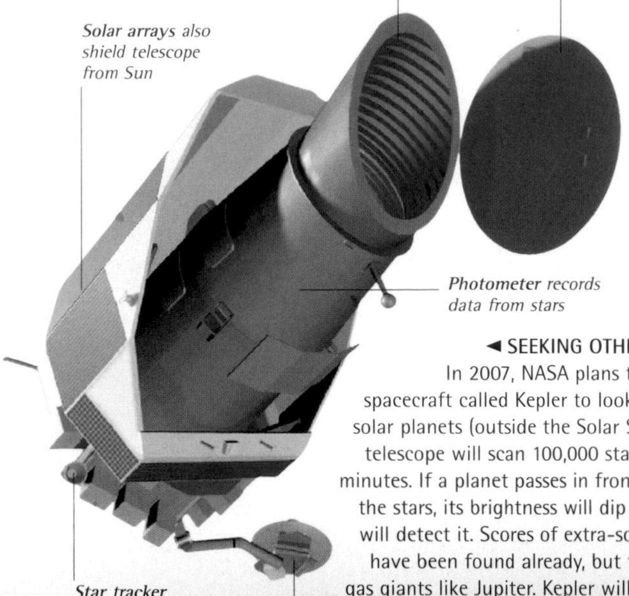

Sunshade stops sunlight entering telescope

Deployable cover

Solar arrays also shield telescope from Sun

Photometer records data from stars

Star tracker

Antenna beams images and data to Earth once a week

◄ SEEKING OTHER EARTHS
In 2007, NASA plans to launch a spacecraft called Kepler to look for extra-solar planets (outside the Solar System). Its telescope will scan 100,000 stars every 15 minutes. If a planet passes in front of any of the stars, its brightness will dip and Kepler will detect it. Scores of extra-solar planets have been found already, but they are all gas giants like Jupiter. Kepler will be able to detect small Earth-like planets.

Three towers and 18 cables support the 1,000-tonne platform

Arecibo's dish reflects radio waves to and from space

ARECIBO RADIO TELESCOPE ►
Arecibo is the world's most sensitive radio telescope. Astronomers use it to study radio signals from distant stars and galaxies. SETI scientists scan about 1,000 stars for any radio signals that might be artificial, as these may come from extraterrestrial beings. The 305-m (1,000-ft) dish lies in a natural hollow on the Caribbean island of Puerto Rico. The reflector's surface is made of 40,000 aluminium panels.

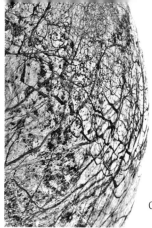

◄ EUROPA
Jupiter's moon Europa is about the same size as Earth's Moon, but Europa is covered with ice. Lines as long as 3,000 km (1,850 miles) on its surface look like cracks in the ice. Scientists think there may be a liquid ocean underneath. If it contains water, there may be life there, too. In 2012, NASA is planning to send the Jupiter Icy Moons Orbiter to scan Europa and two other moons, Granymede and Callisto, which may harbour oceans beneath ice.

PAST LIFE ►

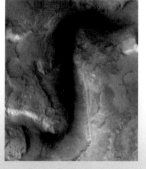

Photographs of Mars taken by orbiting spacecraft show features that look very similar to riverbeds and flood plains on Earth that were formed by flowing water. The Mars Exploration Rovers have found layered rocks that look like sea-bed sediments. These features suggest that water did flow on Mars long ago. This means that even if Mars is a dead planet today, scientists may be able to find evidence of past life in its rocks, or even micro-organisms living below the dead surface.

SENDING MESSAGES ►
In 1974, the Arecibo radio telescope transmitted a coded message towards the M13 star cluster. M13 contains 300,000 stars and lies near the edge of our galaxy, 21,000 light years away. The message consisted of 1,679 bits of information. If intelligent beings receive the code, they should be able to rearrange it into 73 lines of 23 bits. In this form, it shows a series of shapes, including the Arecibo dish, our solar system, and a human. If life forms do work it out, a return message would take about 48,000 years to get here from M13.

Binary code gives the numbers one to ten

Symbols represent the chemicals hydrogen, carbon, oxygen, nitrogen, and phosphorus

Twisted lines stand for DNA, the molecule that passes on the blueprint of life

Human figure and Earth's population

Solar system, with Earth out of line to highlight it

Arecibo radio telescope with radio waves

ET life

Dome contains reflectors that focus radio waves onto antennae

SETI AT HOME

Millions of home computer users all over the world have joined the search for extraterrestrial intelligence. Data from the Arecibo telescope is divided up into smaller units and sent to home computer users running software called SETI@Home. Their screensavers analyse data received from the telescope and send it back to the SETI headquarters. The software looks for very narrow-band radio signals, which are most unlikely to come from natural sources. These would show up as spikes flickering on the screen.

◄ ION ENGINE

Smart-1 was launched in 2003 to orbit and map the Moon. In orbit, this spacecraft is powered by an ion engine, not rocket fuel. Its solar panels convert sunlight into electricity, which is used to give gas atoms an electric charge. The charged atoms are then made to speed away from the spacecraft, pushing the craft in the opposite direction. Although less powerful than a rocket, an ion engine can gently propel a spacecraft for months or years.

Spacecraft powered by an ion engine

Engine nozzle concentrates gas jet

Blue glow of gas jetting from the engine

Solar panel converts sunlight into electricity

THE FUTURE IN SPACE

Scientists and engineers are planning new manned and unmanned space missions for the future. In 2004, US President George W. Bush announced that the USA intends to send astronauts back to the Moon by 2020 and to Mars after that. One of the most exciting unmanned missions will search for signs of life on Earth-like planets orbiting other stars. Looking further into the future, spacecraft will need new engines that improve on the fuels and rockets used today. One of these, the ion engine, has already been test-flown on several unmanned missions.

▲ MOON BASE

Robots such as the rovers that have been put on the Moon and Mars have been a great success, but some scientists think that human exploration is much more effective. It is likely that humans will return to the Moon in the 21st century. After that, the next stop is Mars. If astronauts do one day make the six-month flight to Mars, separate cargo craft will probably already have delivered supplies for them, together with a module to live in.

Heat radiator sheds excess heat into space

Communications antenna sends and receives radio signals

◄ NUCLEAR POWER

Spacecraft sent beyond the orbit of Mars cannot use solar panels to make electricity, because there is not enough sunlight. Future missions to the outer Solar System may use nuclear-powered craft. The spacecraft for the proposed Jupiter Icy Moons Orbiter mission will be propelled by ion engines powered by electricity from a nuclear generator. The generator will also provide electricity for the spacecraft's science experiments.

Science package contains science experiments

Boom separates the reactor from the science package

Jupiter's moon Europa will have its icy surface probed

Thruster pod houses an ion engine

Radar antenna probes below the surface of moons

Each sail could be several kilometres across

Sails unfurl to catch sunlight

Spacecraft does not need large fuel tanks

Power conversion system changes nuclear energy into electricity

Shielding surrounds the reactor's radioactive material

SOLAR SAILS ▲

Sunlight itself can propel a spacecraft. When sunlight strikes something, it gives a tiny push. The effect is so small that it is not noticed normally – but if the sunlight strikes a big enough surface, the tiny pushes all over it add up to something big enough to move a spacecraft. Spacecraft propelled by sunlight would have giant sails of a paper-thin material. The acceleration produced by the sunlight would be small – but it would be constant, so over time the craft could be boosted to very high speeds.

▲ DOUBLE STAR

The Double Star mission is a joint project between the European Space Agency and the Chinese National Space Administration to study the Sun's effect on Earth. It is called Double Star because there are two spacecraft. One is orbiting close to Earth's equator and the other will orbit its poles. Some time after June 2004, they will start working together and also with four Cluster satellites already in orbit. Data from the satellites will be beamed down to ground stations in Spain and China.

future

Solar panels supply power to operate each telescope

Each telescope will be 1.5 m (5 ft) in diameter

DARWIN ▶

The Darwin mission will use a fleet of space telescopes to look for life on planets orbiting distant stars. This is a big challenge, because the light from a star swamps nearby planets and makes them hard to see. A telescope 30 m (100 ft) across is needed, but it is impossible to launch such a big telescope. Six smaller telescopes will work together as if they were one big telescope. They will look for tell-tale changes in each planet's atmosphere caused by life.

Telescope is cooled to -265˚C (-445˚F)

SPACE TIMELINE

The Space Age began in 1957, although the rocket technology underlying space travel can be traced back to some key developments earlier in the 20th century. Since 1957, virtually every year has seen significant developments in space exploration.

1926 Robert H. Goddard launches the first liquid-fuelled rocket.

1944 The V-2 rocket, from which all modern space rockets are derived, is developed by Germany as a weapon towards the end of World War II.

1957 Soviet Union launch Sputnik 1, the first artificial satellite.

Laika is the first dog in space, travelling aboard the Sputnik 2 satellite.

1958 First US artificial satellite, Explorer 1, is launched.

1959 The Soviet space probe Luna 1 is the first to leave Earth orbit.

Luna 2 is the first space probe to reach the surface of a celestial object – the Moon.

Luna 3 probe returns the first photographs of the far side of the Moon.

The first seven American astronauts, called the Mercury Seven, are selected.

1960 The first weather satellite, TIROS-1, is launched.

The Soviet Union puts two dogs, Strelka and Belka, into space and returns them safely.

1961 The first manned spaceflight by the Soviet cosmonaut Yuri Gagarin in the Vostok 1 spacecraft.

First US manned spaceflight by Alan Shepard in the Mercury 3 spacecraft.

American President John F. Kennedy announces America's intention to land humans on the Moon by the end of the 1960s.

The Soviet space probe, Venera 1, is the first to fly by Venus, although contact with it is lost before it reaches Venus.

1962 The first US manned orbital spaceflight, Mercury 6, with John Glenn on board.

First successful communications satellite, Telstar 1, sends the first direct TV pictures from USA to Europe.

The pop record *Telstar*, by the Tornadoes, climbs to number one in the singles charts in both the UK and US.

The US space probe Mariner 2 flies by Venus and sends back data about the planet.

1963 Valentina Tereshkova becomes the first woman to fly in space, aboard the Vostok 6.

1964 First three-person spacecraft, Voskhod 1, is launched.

Ranger 7, a US space probe, crash-lands into the Moon, giving the first high-resolution mages of the lunar surface.

1965 First spacewalk, by a crew member (Alexei Leonov) of the Soviet spacecraft, Voskhod 2.

The first US two-person spaceflight, Gemini 3.

The US space probe Mariner 4 flies by Mars, the first spacecraft ever successfully to do so.

1966 First soft-landing of a spacecraft on the Moon, the Soviet craft Luna 9.

NASA launches the first Earth observation satellite, ESSA-1.

Both the Soviet Union and the US put space probes, Luna 10 and Lunar Orbiter 1, into orbit around the Moon.

The first American soft-landing on the Moon, by the Surveyor 1 space probe.

1967 Fire during Apollo 1 ground test kills three astronauts.

First test-flight of the Saturn V rocket, launching the unmanned Apollo 4 spacecraft.

The Soviet space probe Venera 4 is the first to descend through the atmosphere of Venus and send back data.

Vladimir Komarov dies during re-entry of the Soyuz 1 spacecraft.

1968 The first US three-man spaceflight, Apollo 7.

First manned spacecraft to leave Earth and orbit the Moon, Apollo 8.

The film *2001: A Space Odyssey* is released; though many are baffled by the plot, it gives a scientifically accurate picture of various aspects of living and travelling in space.

1969 Two Apollo 11 astronauts are the first humans to walk on the surface of the Moon.

A second Moon landing is made by two Apollo 12 astronauts.

1970 An explosion occurs aboard the Apollo 13 spacecraft as it travels to the Moon, but the crew of three return safely to Earth.

The Soviet space probe Venera 7 is the first to make a controlled landing on Venus.

Luna 16 is the first robotic space probe to land on the Moon, take a sample, and send it back to Earth.

The Soviet robotic vehicle Lunokhod is landed on the Moon and begins to explore.

China and Japan launch their first artificial satellites.

1971 The first space station, Salyut 1, is launched by the Soviet Union.

Three cosmonauts die during re-entry of Soyuz 11 after becoming the first crew to live on a space station.

The US space probe Mariner 9 becomes the first human-built object to orbit Mars, where it detects huge volcanoes and deep canyons on the planet's surface.

1972 The Soviet probe Mars 2 is the first human-made object to reach the surface of Mars.

NASA launches Pioneer 10, the first space probe to travel to the outer planets.

Last Apollo moon-landing, Apollo 17.

First Earth Resources Technology Satellite, ERTS, is launched.

1973 First US space station, Skylab, is put in orbit.

Pioneer 10 is the first space probe to fly past Jupiter and take close-up pictures of the planet and some of its moons.

1974 The US probe Mariner 10 is the first space probe to fly past the planet Mercury.

1975 The Soviet space probe Venera 9 is the first to send pictures back from the surface of Venus.

The United States and the Soviet Union cooperate in space for the first time when an Apollo craft docks with a Soviet Soyuz craft.

1976 Two US space probes, Viking 1 and Viking 2, land on Mars, send back numerous pictures of the planet's surface, and look for life.

1977 Voyager 2, the only space probes to visit four planets (Jupiter, Saturn, Uranus, and Neptune), is launched, closely followed by Voyager 1.

1978 The first of 24 Global Positioning System navigation satellites is put in Earth orbit.

Czech Vladimir Remek becomes the first non-American, non-Soviet citizen to fly in space.

1979 Pioneer 11 is the first space probe to pass by Saturn and take close-up photographs of its rings.

First launch of Europe's Ariane rocket.

The Voyager 1 and Voyager 2 space probes fly by Jupiter and return dramatic pictures of the planet, its rings, and some of its larger moons.

1980 The Voyager 1 probe sends back pictures of Saturn, revealing it has thousands of ringlets.

The Pioneer Venus 1 probe discovers mountains higher than Mount Everest on Venus.

1981 The first US Space Shuttle mission, Columbia, STS-1.

1982 The last Russian Salyut space station, Salyut 7, is launched.

1983 The world's first infrared astronomical satellite, called IRAS, is launched.

Dr. Sally Ride becomes the first American woman in space on board the Space Shuttle Challenger.

First Spacelab flies on the Space Shuttle.

Pioneer 10 becomes the first object made by humans to leave the Solar System.

US President Ronald Reagan announces the Strategic Defence Initiative, a space-based system designed to defend the USA from attack by nuclear missiles; it is dubbed Star Wars by opponents.

1984 The first untethered spacewalks are made by Space Shuttle astronauts, using manned manoeuvring units.

1986 The first part of the Russian Mir space station is launched.

Space Shuttle Orbiter Challenger explodes just after launch, with loss of all seven of its crew members.

The Japanese space probes Suisei and Sakigake make successful fly-bys of Halley's comet.

European Space Agency Giotto probe makes a successful fly-by of Halley's comet.

Voyager 2 space probe flies past Uranus, returning pictures of the planet, its numerous rings, and moons.

1989 Voyager 2 flies past Neptune, returning pictures of the planet, its rings, and moons.

1990 Magellan space probe begins to orbit the planet Venus and maps its surface.

Hubble Space Telescope is launched.

1991 European Remote Sensing satellite (ERS-1), Europe's first environmental satellite, goes into orbit.

The Soviet Union breaks up and is partially replaced by a Commonwealth of Independent States (CIS), consisting of Russia and ten smaller countries. The former Soviet Union's space programme effectively becomes Russia's space programme.

1992 The ESA/NASA space probe Ulysses swings by Jupiter and goes into an orbit that will take it over both of the Sun's poles.

The COBE satellite maps the cosmic microwave background radiation for the first time.

1994 Ulysses space probe makes first flight over the Sun's poles.

1995 Galileo space probe goes into orbit around Jupiter.

Russian cosmonaut Valeri Poliakov returns to Earth after spending a record 438 days in space, aboard the Mir space station.

The Solar and Heliospheric Observatory mission (SOHO) is launched into a solar orbit.

1996 NASA confirms that water has been detected on the Moon by the Lunar Prospector spacecraft.

The French satellite Cerise is the first to collide with a catalogued piece of space junk.

1997 NASA's Pathfinder space probe lands on Mars and releases the Sojourner rover onto the planet's surface.

1998 First part of the International Space Station is launched.

1999 The powerful Chandra X-ray Observatory is launched into Earth orbit by the Space Shuttle Columbia.

2000 Two Russian cosmonauts and an American astronomer become the first occupants of the International Space Station.

2001 NEAR-Shoemaker is the first space probe to be landed on an asteroid, Eros.

The Mir space station burns up in Earth's atmosphere after 15 years in orbit.

NASA's Deep space 1 probe successfully flies by comet Borrelly.

2002 Mars Odyssey spacecraft starts mapping the planet Mars and looks for water.

2003 Space Shuttle Orbiter Columbia breaks up and is destroyed when re-entering Earth's atmosphere, with loss of all seven of its crew members.

2004 US President George W. Bush announces America's intention to send more astronauts to the Moon by the year 2020 and to use Moon missions as a stepping stone for future space exploration.

Stardust spacecraft flies through the coma of Comet Wild 2 and captures thousands of fresh cometary dust particles.

Spirit and Opportunity rovers successfully land on the surface of Mars.

Cassini-Huygens space probe scheduled to go into orbit around Saturn.

2005 Deep Impact probe scheduled to encounter Comet 9P/Tempel 1.

2006 Mars Reconnaissance Orbiter mission is scheduled to reach the planet Mars.

2011 NASA's Messenger space probe is scheduled to start orbiting the planet Mercury.

2012 European Space agency's BepiColombo spacecraft, which includes two Mercury orbiters, is scheduled for launch.

2014 European Space Agency's Rosetta space probe is scheduled to encounter the comet 67P/Churyumov-Gerasimenko and put a small lander on its surface.

MOON LANDING SITES

More than 55 spacecraft have reached the Moon since 1959. Some flew by it, went into orbit around it, or orbited it and then returned to Earth. Below is a summary of 19 of the more important missions that have actually landed or crash-landed on the Moon up to 2004.

maps

(1) LUNA 2 (USSR)

Landing date: 14 September 1959
Location: Near Autolycus crater
Details: The first spacecraft to land on any object outside Earth, though it crash-landed.

(2) AND (3) RANGERS 7 AND 8 (USA)

Landing dates: 28 July 1964 and 20 February 1965
Locations: Near Mare Nubium (Sea of Clouds) and Mare Tranquillitatis (Sea of Tranquillity)
Details: Each spacecraft transmitted a series of pictures as it crash-landed on to the Moon.

(4) LUNA 9 (USSR)

Landing date: 3 February 1966
Location: Western side of Oceanus Procellarum (Ocean of Storms)
Details: The first craft to soft-land on any object outside Earth. Luna 9 sent photographs and TV pictures back to Earth for 3 days.

(5) SURVEYOR 1 (USA)

Landing date: 2 June 1966
Location: Near the centre of Oceanus Procellarum (Ocean of Storms)
Details: The first successful soft-landing by a US spacecraft on any object outside Earth. The spacecraft found it had landed in a 2 cm- (1 inch-) thick layer of dust.

(6) LUNA 13 (USSR)

Landing date: 24 December 1966
Location: Western side of Oceanus Procellarum (Ocean of Storms)
Details: As well as returning TV pictures and data, the probe tested the lunar soil's density and measured its radioactivity.

(7) SURVEYOR 3 (USA)

Landing date: 20 April 1967
Location: Eastern side of Oceanus Procellarum (Ocean of Storms)
Details: The probe was the first to carry a surface soil-sampling scoop. Samples were placed in front of the spacecraft's television cameras for image transmission back to Earth.

(8) AND (9) SURVEYORS 5 AND 6 (USA)

Landing dates: 11 September and 10 November 1967
Locations: Mare Tranquillitatis (Sea of Tranquillity) and Sinus Medii (Central Bay)
Details: Performed soil surveys and sent back large numbers of photographs to Earth.

(10) APOLLO 11 (USA)

Landing date: 20 July 1969
Location: Western side of Mare Tranquillitatis (Sea of Tranquillity)
Astronauts: Neil Armstrong and "Buzz" Aldrin
Details: The first mission in which humans walked on the lunar surface. During their 21.5-hour stay on the Moon, Armstrong and Aldrin walked a distance of about 250 m (800 ft), set up scientific experiments, took photographs, and collected lunar samples.

(11) APOLLO 12 (USA)

Landing date: 19 November 1969
Location: Eastern side of Oceanus Procellarum (Ocean of Storms)
Astronauts: "Pete" Conrad and Alan Bean
Details: Conrad and Bean set up scientific experiments, examined the nearby Surveyor 3 spacecraft, collected lunar samples, and took photographs during two moonwalks. Their stay on the Moon lasted 31.5 hours.

(12) LUNA 16 (USSR)

Landing date: 17 September 1970
Location: Mare Fecunditatis (Sea of Fertility)
Details: This probe drilled into the Moon's surface, took a sample, and then successfully sent the sample back to Earth.

(13) LUNA 17 (USSR)

Landing date: 17 November 1970
Location: Mare Imbrium (Sea of Rains)
Details: Delivered the first Lunokhod rover to the Moon's surface. Lunokhod journeyed over the Moon's surface for 10 months and returned over 20,000 photographs.

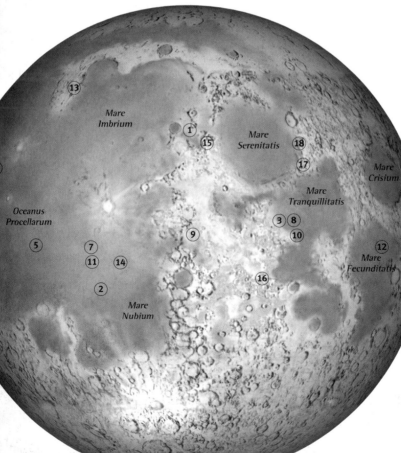

NEAR SIDE OF MOON

APOLLO 14 (USA)

Landing date: 5 February 1971
Location: Fra Mauro region
Astronauts: Alan Shepard and Edgar Mitchell
Details: During their stay on the Moon, the two astronauts set up science experiments, collected Moon rocks, and took photographs. Shepard hit two golf balls. Their stay on the Moon lasted for 33.5 hours.

(15) APOLLO 15 (USA)

Landing date: 30 July 1971
Location: Hadley Rille highland region
Astronauts: David Scott and James Irwin
Details: During their 67-hour stay on the Moon, Scott and Irwin made three extra-vehicular activities (EVAs) or Moon explorations. This was the first mission to employ the Lunar Roving Vehicle, which was used to explore regions within 5 km (3 miles) of the landing site.

(16) APOLLO 16 (USA)

Landing date: 20 April 1972
Location: Descartes highland region
Astronauts: John Young and Charles Duke
Details: During their 3-day stay on the Moon,. Young and Duke made three EVAs (Moon explorations). They drove 27 km (16 miles) using the Lunar Roving Vehicle, collected 95 kg (210 lb) of rock and soil samples, took photographs, and set up scientific experiments.

(17) APOLLO 17 (USA)

Landing date: 11 December 1972
Location: Taurus-Littrow region
Astronauts: Eugene Cernan and Harrison Schmitt
Details: Schmitt, the first scientist on the Moon, and Cernan made three EVAs (Moon explorations) totalling over 22 hours. During this time they covered 30 km (18 miles) in the Lunar Roving Vehicle, and collected 110.5 kg (243 lb) of rocks and dust. The total duration of their stay on the Moon was 75 hours.

(18) LUNA 21 (USSR)

Landing date: 15 January 1973
Location: Mare Serenitatis (Sea of Serenity)
Details: Delivered the Lunokhod 2 lunar rover, which journeyed over the Moon's surface for a total of 4 months.

(19) LUNAR PROSPECTOR (USA)

Landing date: 31 July 1999
Location: A shadowed crater not far from the Moon's south pole
Details: It was hoped that the impact of the probe would liberate water vapour from suspected ice deposits in the crater and that the plume would be detectable from Earth. However, no plume was observed.

MARS LANDING SITES

The 10 spacecraft listed below are the only ones that have landed, or are thought to have landed, on Mars up to 2004. Others have flown by Mars or gone into orbit around it.

maps

(1) MARS 2 (USSR)

Landing date: 27 November 1971
Location: Hellas Planitia
Details: Crash-landed while a dust storm was raging on the surface of Mars.

(2) MARS 3 (USSR)

Landing date: 2 December 1971
Location: Near Terra Sirenum
Details: Soft-landed and operated for 20 seconds before failing, possibly due to a dust storm on Mars. One dark, fuzzy image of the Martian surface was returned.

(3) MARS 6 (USSR)

Landing date: 12 March 1974
Location: Margaritifer Sinus region
Details: Communication with lander craft was lost just before landing.

(4) VIKING 1 (USA)

Landing date: 20 July 1976
Location: Chryse Planitia
Details: Soft-landed and transmitted images of the Martian surface, took soil samples, and chemically analysed them for composition and signs of life. Viking 1 also studied Mars' atmosphere and weather, and deployed Marsquake-measuring devices. Communications ended on 13 November 1982.

(5) VIKING 2 (USA)

Landing date: 3 September 1976
Location: Near Utopia Planitia
Details: Very similar to the Viking 1 mission (above) except for the location and the fact that communications ended on 11 April 1980.

(6) MARS PATHFINDER (USA)

Landing date: 4 July 1997
Location: Chryse Planitia
Details: After a soft-landing, the Pathfinder lander deployed a small rover (Sojourner) and made measurements of conditions on Mars. The lander returned almost 10,000 images. The rover explored the Martian surface, analysed rocks and soil, and returned a total of 550 images. Communications ended on 27 September 1997.

(7) MARS POLAR LANDER (USA)

Landing date: 3 December 1999
Location: Towards the south pole of Mars
Details: Contact with the lander was lost as it began the final stages of its descent.

(8) BEAGLE 2 (EUROPEAN SPACE AGENCY)

Landing date: 25 December 2003
Location: Isidis Planitia
Details: Declared lost after no communications were received following the scheduled landing.

(9) SPIRIT ROVER (USA)

Landing date: 4 January 2004
Location: Gusev crater
Details: After a successful soft-landing, began exploring Mars. The mission's main goal was to search for and analyse rocks and soils that may hold clues to past water activity on Mars.

(10) OPPORTUNITY ROVER (USA)

Landing date: 25 January 2004
Location: Meridiani Planum
Details: Mission goal was the same as for Spirit rover; soon found direct evidence for the existence of past water on surface of Mars.

WESTERN HEMISPHERE OF MARS

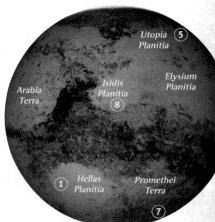

EASTERN HEMISPHERE OF MARS

SPACE TRAVEL BIOGRAPHIES

These biographies provide short descriptions of the lives of some notable people who have travelled in space (selected from a total of well over 400 who have been in space since 1961) or were important pioneers of spaceflight science and technology.

biographies

EDWIN "BUZZ" ALDRIN   *born 1930*

Known by the childhood nickname Buzz, Edwin Aldrin was the second person ever to walk on the Moon. As the pilot of Apollo 11's lunar module, he stepped onto the lunar surface 19 minutes after Neil Armstrong on 21 July 1969. Born in New Jersey, Aldrin took a degree in engineering and then became a pilot with the US Air Force. After further studies in astronautics, Aldrin was selected for astronaut training in 1963. Before his trip to the Moon, he had made a record 2½-hour spacewalk during the Gemini 12 mission. Aldrin retired from NASA in 1971 and became one of the world's leading advocates of space exploration through writing and public speaking.

NEIL ARMSTRONG   *born 1930*

Neil Armstrong achieved worldwide fame for being the first person to step onto the Moon, as the commander of Apollo 11, at 2.56 am Greenwich Mean Time on 21 July 1969. Born in Ohio, Armstrong had flying lessons as a teenager and gained his pilot's licence before he was legally old enough to drive a car. He studied aeronautical engineering at college, became a Navy fighter pilot, and later a test pilot for NASA. Armstrong made his first spaceflight as command pilot for Gemini 8 in 1966, and three years later made his historic voyage to the Moon. A lunar crater close to the Apollo 11 landing site is named after him in his honour. Armstrong left NASA in 1971 and became a university professor before going into business.

SERGEI AVDEYEV   *born 1956*

The Russian cosmonaut Sergei Avdeyev holds the record for the most time spent in space, with 748 days accumulated on three flights in the 1990s. Born in Chapayevsk in south central European Russia, Avdeyev graduated in 1979 from the Moscow Institute as an engineer-physicist. In 1987 he was selected for cosmonaut training. His three spaceflights were as a flight engineer aboard the Mir space station in 1992-1993, 1995-1996, and 1998-1999. His body has been examined and monitored many times over by doctors researching the consequences of space travel.

EUGENE CERNAN   *born 1934*

Eugene Cernan is best known for being the last person to have stood on the Moon, as commander of Apollo 17 in 1972. Born in Chicago, Cernan took a degree in engineering before becoming a US Navy pilot. NASA selected him as an astronaut in 1963. His first spaceflight, in 1966, was aboard Gemini 9. On this mission, Cernan became the second American to walk in space. In 1970 Cernan was lunar module pilot on Apollo 10, which travelled to the Moon but did not land. During the Apollo 17 mission, Cernan and his companion Harrison Schmitt set records for the longest time moving around on the lunar surface (over 22 hours) and largest return of lunar rocks (110 kg or 243 lb). Cernan left NASA in 1976 to go into business.

EILEEN COLLINS   *born 1956*

NASA astronaut Eileen Collins was the first woman to command a Space Shuttle mission. Born in New York State, Collins holds several degrees in science, mathematics, economics, and management, and worked as an Air Force pilot before selection for astronaut training in 1990. She has made three Space Shuttle flights, in 1995, 1997, and 1999, the last as Shuttle commander. A highlight of the 1999 mission (Shuttle mission STS-93) was the deployment of a special space telescope (the Chandra X-Ray Observatory), which is designed to help scientists study phenomena such as exploding stars and black holes.

MICHAEL COLLINS   *born 1930*

Michael Collins was one of the three astronauts on the Apollo 11 mission that put the first people on the Moon in 1969. Collins was in charge of the command module Columbia, which stayed in lunar orbit as his colleagues, Neil Armstrong and Edwin "Buzz" Aldrin, visited the Moon's surface. Born in Rome, Italy, Collins graduated from the US Military Academy in 1952 and then became an Air Force test pilot. In 1963 he was selected for astronaut training and in 1966 made his first spaceflight aboard Gemini 10. Collins resigned from NASA the year after his Apollo mission. He worked as a museum director at the Smithsonian Institution in Washington DC and later entered business.

CHARLES "PETE" CONRAD   *1930-1999*

Charles "Pete" Conrad was the third US astronaut to set foot on the Moon, as commander of the Apollo 12 mission in 1969. Born in Philadelphia, Conrad took a degree in aeronautical engineering before becoming a pilot with the US Navy. In 1962 he was selected for astronaut training. As well as his Apollo 12 journey to the Moon, Conrad flew on two Gemini missions (Gemini 5 and Gemini 11) and was commander of Skylab II, the first US Space Station. In 1973 he left NASA to pursue a business career.

MICHAEL FOALE   *born 1957*

British-born Michael Foale holds the record for being the NASA astronaut who has spent longest in space. By the end of April 2004, he had spent a total of 374 days in space, including stints on six Space Shuttle missions, one stay on the Russian space station Mir, and as a commander of the International Space Station. Born in Lincolnshire, England, Foale completed a degree in physics in 1978 and a PhD in astrophysics in 1982. He then moved to Houston, Texas, to work for the US space programme and was selected as an astronaut candidate in 1987. In 1997, he spent 145 days living and working on Mir and narrowly escaped death when an unmanned cargo craft accidentally collided with the space station during a docking test.

YURI GAGARIN   *1934-1968*

The Russian cosmonaut Yuri Gagarin was the first person ever to fly in space, aboard the Vostok 1 spacecraft in 1961. The 108-minute flight, during which he travelled 40,000 km (25,000 miles), was his only trip into space. Born in the village of Klushino in the Smolensk region, Gagarin studied at an industrial college in his teens while learning to fly aeroplanes. In 1957 he became a pilot in the Soviet Air Force, then joined the cosmonaut corps and four years later was chosen as the first person to journey into space. After his spaceflight, Gagarin became internationally famous and a world hero. He received many honours, including the renaming of his home town as Gagarin. He was killed in an aeroplane crash in 1968 while training for another flight.

JOHN GLENN
born 1921

John Glenn was the first American to orbit Earth, aboard the Mercury 6 spacecraft. His flight took him on three orbits of Earth in less than 5 hours. Born in Ohio, Glenn served in the Marine Corps during World War II, and later in Korea. In 1954, he started work as a test pilot and in 1957 made the first nonstop supersonic flight from Los Angeles to New York. In 1959, he was selected for astronaut training, and was back-up pilot for the first two Mercury missions. During his Mercury 6 flight, he became the third American in space and the third person to orbit Earth. After retiring from the space programme in 1964, Glenn took up politics, and in 1974 was elected Senator in Ohio. In 1998, he became the world's oldest astronaut at age 77 when he flew on a Space Shuttle mission.

ROBERT GODDARD
1882-1945

Robert Goddard was an American physicist and rocket engineer who, in 1926, launched the world's first liquid-fuelled rocket. Born in Massachusetts, Goddard became fascinated by the idea of space travel from an early age and, after obtaining a degree in physics, put his mind to developing a space rocket. In 1919 he published his theory of rocketry, and in the 1930s he launched his first stabilized rocket. The US space programme grew out of his pioneering efforts, although his work was largely ignored until after his death. NASA's Goddard Space Flight Center, Maryland, is named after him.

VIRGIL "GUS" GRISSOM
1926-1967

In July 1961, Virgil Grissom became the second American to go into space, aboard the Mercury 4 spacecraft. Four years later, his second space flight aboard Gemini 3 earned him the distinction of being the first person to fly in space twice. Grissom was born in Indiana and after earning a degree in mechanical engineering became a jet pilot who saw action in the Korean War. In 1959 he was selected for astronaut training. His successful flight on Mercury 4 lasted just over 15 minutes. After the capsule splashed down in the Atlantic it started sinking, and Grissom only just managed to swim clear. He died in 1967 as a result of a fire in the Apollo 1 spacecraft.

MAE JEMISON
born 1956

Mae Jemison was the first African-American woman in space, flying aboard the Space Shuttle Endeavour in 1992. Born in Alabama, she has degrees in both chemical engineering and medicine and was working as a doctor in Los Angeles when in 1987 she was selected for astronaut training. She resigned from NASA in 1993, not long after her Space Shuttle mission, and founded an organization committed to the advancement and beneficial uses of space technology and exploration.

SERGEI KOROLEV
1906-1966

Sergei Korolev was a Ukrainian-born designer and engineer who directed the Soviet Union's space programme during its early years. His name is linked with many of the great achievements of the first decades of the space age. He was responsible for the Cosmos, Vostok, and Soyuz series of spacecraft. He also played a key role in the launch of Sputnik 1 (the first satellite in space), the first human spaceflight by Yuri Gagarin, and the first spacewalk, by Alexei Leonov.

ALEXEI LEONOV
born 1934

Alexei Leonov is famous for being the first person to walk in space. Born in Listvyanka, Siberia, Leonov is a former jet pilot and was selected for cosmonaut training in 1960. On 18 March 1965, he was launched into orbit aboard Voskhod 2 along with fellow Russian Pavel Belyayev. During the flight, Leonov spent over 20 minutes outside the capsule. This was longer than originally planned because excess pressure in his spacesuit meant that he had great difficulty re-entering the spacecraft's hatch. Leonov made a second flight 10 years later, making history when his Soyuz craft docked with an American Apollo craft, joining the two nations in space.

YANG LIWEI
born 1965

Yang Liwei was the first Chinese person to travel in space, in 2003 aboard the Shenzhou V spacecraft. Born in China's Liaoning Province, Yang Liwei became an Air Force pilot and was selected for cosmonaut training in 1998. The Shenzhou spacecraft that Yang travelled in, similar to a Soyuz spacecraft, was launched from Jiuquan Satellite Launching Center on 15 October 2003. The successful flight lasted over 21 hours and ended with the re-entry capsule landing the next day on the grasslands of the Gobi Desert, in central Inner Mongolia.

JIM LOVELL
born 1928

Jim Lovell is best known as the commander of the ill-fated Apollo 13 spacecraft, bringing it back to Earth after it had been crippled by an explosion in an oxygen tank on the way to the Moon. Lovell also flew on the Gemini 7 and Gemini 12 missions and the epic six-day journey of Apollo 8 – humanity's maiden voyage to the Moon. Born in Ohio, Lovell spent four years as a test pilot for the US Navy before selection in 1962 for astronaut training. He retired from NASA and the Navy in 1973 and spent several years in business. Lovell was depicted by the actor Tom Hanks in the film *Apollo 13*, based on Lovell's book *Lost Moon: The Perilous Voyage of Apollo 13*. Lovell made a brief appearance at the end of the movie, playing the captain of the recovery ship *USS Iwo Jima*.

SHANNON LUCID
born 1943

American astronaut Shannon Lucid holds the record for the most time spent in space by a woman. In 1996, she spent 188 days in space, living and working aboard the Russian Mir space station. Lucid's total time in space is 223 days. This total includes her Mir mission as well as four Space Shuttle missions. Born in Shanghai, China, Shannon Lucid grew up in Oklahoma, took several science degrees, and worked as a biologist before being selected for astronaut training in 1978.

HERMANN OBERTH
1894-1989

Hermann Oberth was a Romanian-born scientist who pioneered the development of space rocketry. His work on the theories of rocket propulsion and guidance systems in the 1930s resulted in the V-2 rocket. In the 1950s, he worked on the American space programme. Oberth's understanding of the interconnections of fuel consumption, rocket speed, distance and duration of flight, and other factors, helped establish the laws that govern modern rocket flight.

VALERI POLIAKOV
born 1942

The Russian doctor and ex-cosmonaut Valeri Poliakov holds the record for the longest single stay in space, aboard the Mir station, 438 days from 8 January 1994 to 22 March 1995. He also stayed on Mir for 241 days in 1988-1989, and for several years held the record for the most time spent in space. Born in Tula, Russia, Poliakov graduated as a doctor in 1965 and was selected for astronaut training in 1972. In connection with his spaceflights, Poliakov took part in an unusual medical experiment. Before each mission, some of his bone marrow was removed so that it could be compared with another sample of bone marrow taken when he returned after months of weightlessness. Poliakov retired as an astronaut in 1995 and now works for a public health ministry in Moscow.

SALLY RIDE
born 1951

Sally Ride became the first American woman to travel into space in 1983, when she was launched aboard the Space Shuttle Challenger as a mission specialist. Ride's 6-day journey made her the third woman to travel into space (after Valentina Tereshkova in 1963 and Svetlana Savitskaya in 1982). Born in Los Angeles, Ride was a nationally ranked tennis player in her teenage years. A physicist by training, in 1977 she answered a NASA advertisement for Space Shuttle astronauts and was accepted. In addition to her 1983 flight, she made a second Shuttle flight in 1984. Ride helped the movement towards a more equal role for women in the American space programme. In 1987 she left NASA and for many years was a Professor of Physics at the University of California.

HARRISON SCHMITT
born 1935

Harrison Schmitt is famous for being the only scientist to have visited the Moon, as lunar module pilot for the Apollo 17 mission. A geologist by training, Schmitt was born in New Mexico. He was selected by NASA as an astronaut-scientist in 1965. As well as training for space flight, he taught other Apollo crew members how to collect suitable rocks on the Moon and later took part in the analysis of those rocks. Schmitt left NASA in 1975 to enter politics and for six years was a US Senator for New Mexico.

HELEN SHARMAN
born 1963

Helen Sharman was the first British person to travel into space, aboard the Soviet Soyuz TM-12 spacecraft in 1991. Sharman spent 8 days in space, 6 of them aboard the space station Mir. Born in Sheffield, England, she obtained a chemistry degree in 1984, and worked for five years as a research scientist. In 1989, she answered an advertisement: "Astronaut wanted – no experience necessary". Not long afterwards, she found that she had been selected as a trainee cosmonaut for a Soviet space mission. One of the main aspects of her 18-month training programme was to learn Russian. Since her return from space, Helen Sharman has continued to work as a scientist and broadcaster.

ALAN SHEPARD
1923-1998

Alan Shepard was the first American in space, as the occupant of the Mercury 3 spacecraft, which was blasted into space on 5 May 1961. The flight lasted just 15 minutes and did not orbit Earth. Instead, the Mercury capsule landed in the Atlantic Ocean 485 km (300 miles) down range from its launch pad at Cape Canaveral, Florida. Born in New Hampshire, Shepard obtained a degree in aeronautics in 1944 and later became a test pilot for the US Navy. In 1959, he was chosen among the first group of seven American astronauts. As well as his Mercury flight, Shepard was commander of the Apollo 14 mission that landed on the Moon in 1971. During one moonwalk, Shepard famously hit two golf balls for hundreds of yards over the Moon's surface. Shepard retired from NASA in 1974 and went into business.

VALENTINA TERESHKOVA
born 1937

Valentina Tereshkova was the first woman to fly in space. In June 1963, she made 48 Earth orbits aboard the Vostok 6 spacecraft. Born near Yaroslavl in western Russia, Tereshkova left school at 16 to work in a textile factory. She also became an amateur parachutist, and in 1962 was selected for space flight. After her 71-hour Vostok 6 flight, at the end of which Tereshkova parachuted to the ground, she was made a Hero of the Soviet Union. It was to be another 19 years before another woman travelled in space.

DENNIS TITO
born 1940

Dennis Tito is an American multimillionaire who in June 2001 became the world's first space tourist, travelling for 8 days on board the Soyuz TM-32 spacecraft and the International Space Station. During the trip, Tito spent hours gazing at Earth and taking photographs. He paid US $20 million to go on the mission. Born in New York City, Tito earned degrees in astronautics and aeronautics and worked as a scientist at NASA's Jet Propulsion Laboratory before founding an investment management company. After his space journey he described it as a "trip to paradise".

GHERMAN TITOV
1935-2000

Gherman Titov was the second person in space (after Yuri Gagarin), flying on board the Soviet spacecraft Vostok 2, which orbited Earth for 24 hours on 6-7 August 1961. Unlike Gagarin, Titov was briefly allowed to take manual control of his spacecraft during the flight. Born in the Altai region of Siberia, Titov graduated as a Soviet Air Force pilot and was selected for cosmonaut training in 1960. Just short of age 26 at the launch of Vostok 2, he is the youngest person ever to have flown in space. Following his flight, Titov worked in various senior positions in the Soviet Union's space programme until his retirement in 1992. In 1995, he entered politics.

KONSTANTIN TSIOLKOVSKY
1857-1935

Konstantin Tsiolkovsky was a Russian pioneer of the theory of spaceflight. He produced theories of rocketry but did not have the resources to build a rocket. By 1898 he had produced a theory that showed how much fuel a rocket would use and how its velocity was related to the thrust of its engines. He was the first person to propose the use of liquid propellants for rockets. He also worked out that multistage rockets would be needed to leave Earth's gravity and showed how these could be stacked on top of one another.

WERNHER VON BRAUN
1912-1977

Wernher von Braun was a German-born rocket engineer responsible for the development of several important liquid-fuelled rockets in Germany and the USA. During World War II, he led the development of rockets for the German army, in particular the V-2 rocket. Because this was used as a weapon against cities in England, Belgium, France, and the Netherlands, and because thousands of people enslaved by the Nazis were killed while working on von Braun's missile projects, he is a controversial figure. At the end of the war, von Braun and his team surrendered to US forces. The team eventually joined NASA and was responsible for the launch of the first US satellite and for the Saturn V rocket, which was used to launch the Apollo missions to the Moon.

CARL WALZ
born 1955

Carl Walz is co-holder of the record for the longest single US spaceflight. During Expedition 4 of the International Space Station in 2001-2002, he and NASA astronaut Daniel Bursch spent nearly 196 days in space. A veteran of four spaceflights (the other three were Space Shuttle missions), Walz was born in Ohio and trained as a physicist. Selected as an astronaut in 1990, overall he has spent 231 days in space.

EDWARD WHITE
1930-1967

Ed White achieved fame in 1965, when he became the first American to go for a spacewalk, outside of the Gemini 4 spacecraft. White was outside Gemini 4 for 21 minutes, and became the first man to control himself during a spacewalk using a gun filled with compressed gas. When told to return to the spacecraft, White said, "It's the saddest moment of my life". Born in Texas, White took a degree in aeronautical engineering in 1959 and then became an Air Force pilot. He was selected for astronaut training in 1962. White died in 1967, along with Gus Grissom and Roger Chaffee, as a result of a fire in the Apollo 1 spacecraft.

JOHN YOUNG
born 1930

American astronaut John Young was commander of the Apollo 16 mission to the Moon in 1972, the first Space Shuttle flight in 1981, and a second Space Shuttle flight in 1983. He also flew in two Gemini missions (Gemini 3 and 10) during the 1960s, and made 31 lunar orbits in Apollo 10, the dress rehearsal for the first Moon landing. Born in California, Young took a degree in aeronautical engineering before becoming a test pilot in the US Navy. In 1962 he was selected as an astronaut. During the Apollo 16 mission in 1972, Young and Charlie Duke collected some 90 kg (200 lb) of moon rocks and drove over 25 km (16 miles) in a lunar rover on three separate explorations. John Young continues to work for NASA and, as an active astronaut, remains eligible to command future Space Shuttle missions. In preparation for prime and backup crew positions on 11 spaceflights, it is calculated that Young has spent more than 15,000 hours in astronaut training, mostly in simulators and simulations.

GLOSSARY

Terms in *italics* are other glossary entries.

Airlock A sealed chamber in which air pressure can be changed. Astronauts use an airlock to transfer between a pressurized spacecraft and the airless environment of space.

Antenna A device used to send and receive radio signals between a spacecraft and a ground station on Earth or another spacecraft.

Atmosphere A layer of gas held around a planet or moon by its *gravity*.

Celestial object Any object in space, such as a planet, asteroid, moon, *star*, or *galaxy*.

Communications satellite An artificial *satellite* that is used for transferring TV, radio, or telephone signals from one place to another.

Cosmonaut An astronaut from the former Soviet Union or present-day Russia.

Dock To link up one spacecraft with another.

Electromagnetic radiation A form of energy that can travel through the *vacuum* of space.

Electromagnetic spectrum A range of different types of *electromagnetic radiation*, including *radio waves*, *infrared radiation*, light, *ultraviolet radiation*, *X-rays*, and gamma rays.

Elliptical orbit An *orbit* in the shape of an ellipse (a stretched or squashed circle).

Environmental satellite A type of artificial *satellite* that monitors aspects of Earth's environment, such as weather patterns.

Extra-vehicular activity (EVA) Any activity in which an astronaut or *cosmonaut* goes outside the spacecraft. Also called a spacewalk.

Fairing The protective aerodynamic casing around a rocket's *payload* during launch.

Force A push or a pull that can change the velocity of an object.

Free-fall A situation in which an object is travelling in space or orbiting a planet or moon and, in the case of a spacecraft and its occupants, the craft's engine is turned off.

Fuel cell A device that produces electrical energy by combining hydrogen and oxygen.

Fly-by An encounter between a *space probe* and a planet, moon, comet, or asteroid in which the probe does not stop to orbit or land.

Galaxy A collection of millions or billions of *stars*, gas, and dust held together by *gravity*.

Gravitational assist A spacecraft's use of a planet or moon's *gravity* to change its speed or direction of travel.

Gravity A *force* that attracts objects together. The higher the *mass* of the objects, and the closer they are, the greater the gravitational attraction between them.

Heat shield A coating of heat-resistant material on the outer shell of a spacecraft.

Infrared radiation A form of invisible *electromagnetic radiation*. Radiant heat is a form of infrared radiation.

Ion An electrically charged atom or group of atoms.

Ion engine A means of propulsion in space that relies on shooting a fast-moving stream of *ions* out of the spacecraft; this moves the craft itself in the opposite direction.

JPL The Jet Propulsion Laboratory, a part of *NASA* that operates unmanned spacecraft.

Lander A part of a *space probe* designed to land on a planet, moon, asteroid, or comet.

Light year The distance travelled by light through a *vacuum* in a year, about 9.5 million million km (5.9 million million miles).

Lunar Related to the Moon. Being in lunar *orbit* means being in orbit around the Moon.

Magnetic field Magnetism generated by a planet, *star*, or *galaxy*, that extends into space.

Magnetometer A scientific instrument used to detect and study the *magnetic fields* of planets and other *celestial objects*.

Manned manoeuvring unit A special jet backpack used by some astronauts to help them move around in space.

Mass The amount of matter an object contains, measured in kilograms or pounds.

Micrometeoroid shield A protective casing on the outside of a spacecraft, designed to reduce damage caused by the impact of small objects travelling at high speed through space.

Microgravity A state of almost total *weightlessness* experienced when in *free-fall*.

NASA The National Aeronautics and Space Administration, an agency responsible for the USA's civilian space programme.

Orbit The curved path of one object around another under the influence of *gravity*.

Orbiter A spacecraft designed to go into *orbit* around Earth or another *celestial object*.

Payload The cargo that a rocket or shuttle carries into *orbit*, such as an artificial *satellite* or a scientific instrument.

Radar A method of detecting the position and motion of a distant object by using a narrow beam (or pulses) of *radio waves*, which are transmitted to and reflected from the object.

Radio telescope A type of telescope that detects *radio waves* instead of light.

Radiothermal Describes a power source that uses some radioactive material to produce heat, which is then converted into electricity.

Radio wave A form of invisible *electromagnetic radiation*. As well as being used for space communications, radio waves are emitted by various types of *celestial object*.

Re-entry The return of a spacecraft into Earth's *atmosphere*.

Remote-sensing satellite An artificial *satellite* that gathers information about Earth by using a variety of sensors.

Retro-rocket A small rocket engine that is fired opposite to a spacecraft's direction of motion, to reduce the craft's speed.

Rover A type of *lander*, or part of a lander, that is designed to move around on the surface of a planet or moon.

Satellite An object in *orbit* around a more massive object. The planets of the *Solar System* are natural satellites of the Sun. Artificial satellites are launched into orbit for purposes of research, observation, or communication.

Simulator A machine that recreates the conditions of spaceflight.

Soft-land A controlled landing of a spacecraft onto the surface of a planet or other solid *celestial object*.

Solar array See *Solar panel*.

Solar panel A surface covered in devices that convert light into electrical energy.

Solar System The Sun and all the objects that orbit the Sun, such as planets and asteroids.

Solar wind A continuous outflow of charged particles radiating from the Sun.

Space probe A spacecraft sent from Earth to explore other parts of the *Solar System*.

Star A hot, massive, ball of gas whose energy output is produced by nuclear reactions.

Star tracker A camera system linked to a computer that can help a spacecraft navigate by reference to *star* positions.

Suborbital The path of an object that leaves and then re-enters the *atmosphere* without going into *orbit*.

Supernova The massive explosion of a giant *star* at the end of its life, with release of fantastic amounts of light and other energy.

Thrust A sustained *force* in a particular direction produced by a rocket.

Thruster A small rocket used by spacecraft for manoeuvring.

Ultraviolet radiation A form of invisible *electromagnetic radiation*.

Vacuum A region containing no matter. Most of space is a vacuum or a near-vacuum.

Weightlessness A condition in which an astronaut or *cosmonaut* or the contents of a spacecraft seem no longer to be affected by *gravity*, because they are in *free-fall*.

X-ray A form of invisible *electromagnetic radiation*. Certain types of high-energy, very hot *celestial objects* emit X-rays.

INDEX

A page number in **bold** refers to the main entry for that subject.

ACKNOWLEDGEMENTS

Dorling Kindersley would like to thank Alyson Lacewing for proof-reading; Sue Lightfoot for the index; Jenny Siklos for Americanization; Tony Cutting for DTP support; and ILC Dover Inc. for information on space suits for the Space Shuttle..

Dorling Kindersley Ltd is not responsible and does not accept liability for the availability or content of any web site other than its own, or for any exposure to offensive, harmful, or inaccurate material that may appear on the Internet. Dorling Kindersley Ltd will have no liability for any damage or loss caused by viruses that may be downloaded as a result of looking at and browsing the web sites that it recommends. Dorling Kindersley downloadable images are the sole copyright of Dorling Kindersley Ltd, and may not be reproduced, stored, or transmitted in any form or by any means for any commercial or profit-related purpose without prior written permission of the copyright owner.

Picture Credits
The publisher would like to thank the following for their kind permission to reproduce their photographs:

Abbreviations key:
t-top, b-bottom, r-right, l-left, c-centre, a-above, f-far

1 NASA: c. **2** NASA: c. **3** NASA: c. **6–7** NASA. **7** NASA: cl. **8** Corbis: Roger Ressmeyer bc. DK Images: cl. Galaxy Picture Library: tl. **8** Science Photo Library: Californian Association for Research in Astronomy cr; **8–9** Science Photo Library: Detlev Van Ravenswaay c; Frank Zullo t.
9 NASA: cb, bc. Science Photo Library: Davis Ducros br. **10** NASA: tc, cbl, tcl, tcr. Science Photo Library: European Space Agency tl. **11** NASA: br. Science Photo Library: David Ducros bl. **12** Corbis: Hulton-Deutsch Collection cr. NASA: bl. Novosti (London): tl. **13** Corbis: Bettmann cl. NASA: r. **14** European Space Agency: cfr. **15** NASA: cb. **16** Corbis: Bettmann bcl. NASA: bl. Science Photo Library: David A. Hardy tl; Novosti cfr. **17** Corbis: Bettmann cb. DK Images: Science Museum cfr. Genesis Space Photo Library: cfl. NASA: tr. Science Photo Library: David A. Hardy br. **18** Alamy Images: Carol Dixon bl. **19** European Space Agency: tr, br. **20** NASA: bl, bc, br, bcl. Science Photo Library: Novosti Press Agency cl. **21** NASA: tl, tr, br. **22** Science & Society Picture Library: bl. Smithsonian Institution: tr. **23** NASA: b. Science Photo Library: Novosti Photo Library tl, tc. **24** Corbis: bl. NASA: br. Novosti (London): tl. Science Photo Library: NASA cra; Novosti cr. **25** Corbis: Marc Garanger tr. Genesis Space Photo Library: NASA br. NASA: tl, cr, bl. **26** Corbis: cla; Bettmann tr. Novosti (London): clb. Science Photo Library: Starsem bc. **27** NASA: tr, cr. Science Photo Library: NASA br. **28** NASA: cr, l. **29** Corbis: Bettmann c. NASA: crb, bl, t. **30** NASA: cl, c, bl. **30–31** Corbis: NASA. **31** NASA: tc, tr, c, cr, bc, br. **32** Corbis: Bill Ingalls l. DK Images: NASA cr, br. **33** Genesis Space Photo Library: br. NASA: t. Reuters: bl, bcl, bcr. **34** NASA: crb, bra. Reuters: cr. Science Photo Library: David Campione l; NASA br. **35** Courtesy of Lockheed Martin Aeronautics Company, Palmdale: br. NASA: tr. **36–37** Corbis: pic 10; Bettmann pic 3; Roger Ressmeyer pic 9. NASA: pic 1, pic 11, pic 12, pic 13, pic 14, pic 15, Pic 16, pic 2, pic 4, pic 6, pic
7, pic 8, pic 5. **37** NASA: r. **38** NASA: cfl. **40** Corbis: Bettmann cb; Roger Ressmeyer tr. NASA: bl. **41** NASA: c. Novosti (London): br. **42** European Space Agency: bl. NASA: tl. **43** European Space Agency: cfr. NASA: tr, bc. **44** Science Photo Library: bc; Andrew Syred cbl; Eye of Science bcr; GJLP bl. **44–45** NASA: t. **45** NASA: tr, br. Science Photo Library: bl; Alfred Pasieka br; Susumu Nishinaga bc. **46** NASA: tr, cla, cla, cra, cr, bl, br, bcl, bcr, cal, car, cfl, cfr. **47** NASA: tl, bl, cfl, r. **48** NASA: cal, r. **49** NASA: tl, cra, crb, cfr. **50** Corbis: Bettmann cl. NASA: bl. **50–51** Corbis: NASA. **51** NASA: tc, tr. **52** Corbis: Roger Ressmeyer clb, cb, cbl. **52** NASA: tcr. Topfoto.co.uk: cfl. **52–53** NASA. **53** NASA: clb, bcr. **54** NASA: bl, br, cfl. **54–55** NASA. **55** European Space Agency: br. NASA: cra, bl. **56** NASA: ca, cl, br. **56–57** NASA: t. **57** NASA: tr, cr, bc, br. **58** NASA: bl, bc, tcl. **58–59** NASA. **59** Associated Press: J R Hernandez cbr. NASA: tr, br. **62** Alamy Images: CoverSpot tcr. European Space Agency: tl, cb, bl, car. Nokia: tcl. **62–63** NASA. **63** Corbis: Reuters cr. Northrop Grumman Space Technology: tr. Science Photo Library: GE Astro Space tc, cfr; NASA cl, cbl. **64** Corbis: Bettmann br. **64** NASA: cla, bl. **64–65** Corbis: Bettmann **65** NASA: tl, tr, cra, cb, tcl, tcr. Science Photo Library: European Space Agency br. **66** NASA: tl, ca, cb, bl, br, bcl, cal, car, cbl, clb, cbr. **67** NASA: tl, tr, bl, bc, br, cal, call, car, car, cbl, clb, cbr, crb, tcl, tcr. **68** NASA: cla, clb. **68–69** Science Photo Library: Detlev Van Ravenswaay. **69** Corbis: NASA br. NASA: tc, tr, br. Science Photo Library: NASA cr. **70** NASA: cal, cal, cbl, cbl. Science Photo Library: US Geological Survey cfl, tcr. **70–71** NASA. **71** NASA: tl, cr, br, bcl, bcr, cal, cbl, cbr. Science Photo Library: Chris Butler tr; Space Telescope Science
Institute/NASA cfr. **72** NASA: cra, cr, cb. Science Photo Library: US Geological Survey cfl. **73** NASA: cla, cra, b, cal, car. **74** DK Images: Natural History Museum cr. NASA: tc, cl, crb. Science Photo Library: David Nunuk br; Detlev Van Ravenswaay bl; Francois Gohier bl; John Hopkins University Applied Physics Laboratory ca; Novosti Press Agency br. **75** NASA: tr, clb, cb, crb. Science Photo Library: Roger Harris r. **76** Corbis: Gianni Dagli Orti cb. European Space Agency: clb, bcl. **76** Galaxy Picture Library: cbr, cfl. **76–77** European Space Agency. **77** European Space Agency: ca, cra, car, cbr. **78** NASA: clb, bl, bla. National Space Centre, Leicester: br. Science Photo Library: Detlev Van Ravenswaay tr. **78–79** NASA: b, c. **79** NASA: bl, br, bcl, bcr, t. **82** NASA: car. Science Photo Library: David Parker b. **82–83** Science Photo Library: David Parker. European Space Agency: cal. Galaxy Picture Library: car. NASA: tl. Science Photo Library: David Parker br. **84** European Space Agency: cla, b, tcl. **84–85** NASA. **85** European Space Agency: cl, crb, bc. Science Photo Library: Victor Habbick Visions tr. **86** NASA: l. **87** NASA: r.

Jacket images
Front: NASA: (cfl, cfr, cr); Science Photo Library: NASA (cl). **Spine:** NASA. **Back:** Corbis: Bettmann (cfr); NASA: (cr). Science Photo Library: NASA (cfl, cl).

All other images © Dorling Kindersley.
For further information see:
www.dkimages.com